MASTERING REAL ESTATE INVESTMENT

Strategies for Success in Property
Portfolio Growth

Diana Hardy

TABLE OF CONTENT

CHAPTER 1:

Understanding Real Estate Investment

Real estate investment involves the acquisition, ownership, and management of properties for the purpose of generating income and building wealth. It offers opportunities for passive income, portfolio diversification, and long-term appreciation. Understanding real estate investment entails knowledge of market trends, property valuation, financing options, and risk management strategies. With careful analysis and informed decision-making, investors can leverage real estate as a powerful wealth-building asset class.

1.1 Introduction to Real Estate Investment:

Real estate investment stands as a cornerstone of wealth creation and financial security, offering individuals the opportunity to build robust portfolios and secure passive income streams. In an ever-evolving economic landscape, the allure of real estate transcends generations, attracting seasoned investors and newcomers alike with promises of long-term growth and stability.

At its core, real estate investment revolves around the acquisition, ownership, management, and disposition of physical properties. These properties, ranging from residential homes and apartment complexes to commercial buildings and land parcels, serve as tangible assets with intrinsic value and utility. Unlike ephemeral financial instruments, real estate offers investors a tangible stake in the physical world, providing shelter, facilitating commerce, and contributing to the fabric of communities.

The appeal of real estate investment stems from its multifaceted nature and the myriad benefits it affords investors. First and foremost, real estate serves as a reliable source of passive income through rental revenue. By leasing properties to tenants, investors can generate consistent cash flow streams that endure over time, providing financial stability and security.

Additionally, real estate assets have historically appreciated in value, offering investors the potential for long-term capital appreciation and wealth accumulation.

Unlike volatile financial markets, where asset values can fluctuate unpredictably, real estate values tend to exhibit more stable and predictable growth trajectories, making it an attractive option for investors seeking to preserve and grow their wealth.

Furthermore, real estate investment offers unique tax advantages and portfolio diversification benefits. From tax deductions for mortgage interest and property taxes to the ability to leverage debt financing for property acquisitions, real estate investors enjoy a range of incentives that enhance cash flow and overall investment returns.

1.2 Types of Real Estate Investments

Real estate investment offers a diverse array of opportunities for investors to capitalize on various property types, investment strategies, and market niches. In this section, we explore the different types of real estate investments available, each with its unique characteristics, benefits, and considerations.

I. Residential Real Estate

Residential real estate encompasses properties intended for human habitation, such as single-family homes, condominiums, townhouses, and apartment buildings. Investors can generate rental income by leasing residential properties to tenants, providing a steady source of cash flow. Additionally, residential properties offer the potential for long-term capital appreciation, particularly in high-demand areas with robust rental markets and favorable demographics.

II. Commercial Real Estate

Commercial real estate includes properties used for business purposes, such as office buildings, retail spaces, industrial warehouses, and hospitality properties. Investing in commercial real estate offers opportunities for higher rental yields and long-term lease agreements with corporate tenants. Commercial properties are often valued based on their income-producing potential, making them attractive investments for income-focused investors seeking stable cash flow streams.

III. Multifamily Properties

Multifamily properties, including apartment complexes and residential complexes with multiple rental units, present opportunities for investors to scale their real estate portfolios and diversify their income streams. Investing in multifamily properties allows investors to benefit from economies of scale, lower vacancy risks, and higher rental yields compared to single-family homes. Additionally, multifamily properties offer built-in diversification, as vacancies in one unit can be offset by rental income from other units within the same property.

IV. Commercial Real Estate Investment Trusts (REITs)

Real Estate Investment Trusts (REITs) are publicly traded companies that own, operate, or finance income-producing real estate across various sectors. Investing in REITs provides investors with exposure to a diversified portfolio of real estate assets without the need for direct property ownership. REITs offer liquidity, dividend income, and portfolio diversification benefits, making them popular investment vehicles for both individual and institutional investors.

V. Real Estate Syndication

Real estate syndication involves pooling capital from multiple investors to collectively invest in larger real estate projects, such as apartment complexes, commercial developments, or hotel properties. Syndication allows individual investors to access larger and more lucrative investment opportunities that would otherwise be out of reach. Syndicators, typically experienced real estate professionals, manage the investment process, including property acquisition, management, and disposition, while investors passively contribute capital and share in the profits.

VI. Fix-and-Flip Properties

Fix-and-flip investing involves purchasing distressed or undervalued properties, renovating or improving them, and selling them for a profit within a relatively short period. This strategy requires careful market analysis, renovation expertise, and effective project management to maximize returns. Fix-and-flip investors capitalize on market inefficiencies, property value appreciation, and demand for updated or renovated homes in desirable neighborhoods.

VII. Land Investments

Investing in land involves acquiring undeveloped or underutilized parcels of land for future development or appreciation. Land investments offer potential for long-term capital appreciation, strategic development opportunities, and portfolio diversification benefits. Investors may capitalize on land investments through rezoning, entitlements, or selling to developers for residential, commercial, or mixed-use projects.

In summary, the world of real estate investment is vast and diverse, offering investors a plethora of opportunities to achieve their financial goals and build wealth. By understanding the different types of real estate investments available and their respective advantages and considerations, investors can make informed decisions and tailor their investment strategies to align with their objectives and risk tolerance levels.

1.3 Benefits of Investing in Real Estate

Real estate investment offers a multitude of advantages that make it an attractive avenue for building wealth, generating passive income, and achieving financial security. In this section, we explore the various benefits of investing in real estate and how they contribute to the overall appeal of this asset class.

I. Passive Income Generation

One of the most significant benefits of investing in real estate is the ability to generate passive income through rental revenue. By acquiring properties and leasing them to tenants, investors can enjoy a steady and predictable stream of cash flow without the need for active involvement in day-to-day operations. This passive income provides financial stability, supports lifestyle flexibility, and serves as a reliable source of ongoing revenue.

II. Potential for Long-Term Capital Appreciation

Real estate assets have historically demonstrated the potential for long-term capital appreciation, with property values typically increasing over time. Factors such as population growth, urbanization, and economic development contribute to the appreciation of real estate assets, leading to wealth accumulation for investors. Additionally, leveraging strategies such as mortgage financing can amplify returns and accelerate wealth creation through property appreciation.

III. Hedge Against Inflation

Real estate investment serves as a hedge against inflation, as property values and rental income tend to increase in tandem with rising prices. Unlike financial assets such as cash or bonds, which may lose value in inflationary environments, real estate assets have intrinsic value and utility that can withstand inflationary pressures. As a result, real estate investments help preserve the purchasing power of capital over the long term, protecting investors against the erosion of wealth caused by inflation.

IV. Tax Advantages and Incentives

Real estate investment offers a range of tax advantages and incentives that can enhance overall investment returns and maximize cash flow. Mortgage interest deductions, property tax deductions, and depreciation allowances are just a few examples of the tax benefits available to real estate investors. Additionally, strategies such as 1031 exchanges and opportunity zone investments provide opportunities for tax deferral and capital gains reduction, further incentivizing investment in real estate assets.

V. Portfolio Diversification

Real estate investment serves as a valuable component of diversified investment portfolios, offering low correlation with traditional asset classes such as stocks and bonds. By adding real estate assets to their investment portfolios, investors can reduce overall portfolio risk and enhance long-term returns. Furthermore, real estate investments often exhibit resilience during economic downturns, providing a hedge against market volatility and economic uncertainty.

In summary, investing in real estate offers a range of compelling benefits, including passive income generation, potential for long-term capital appreciation, inflation hedging, tax advantages, and portfolio diversification. By leveraging these advantages, investors can build wealth, achieve financial independence, and secure a prosperous future for themselves and their families.

1.4 Market Analysis and Trends

Understanding the real estate market and identifying emerging trends are essential aspects of successful real estate investment. In this section, we delve into the importance of market analysis and trends in guiding investment decisions and maximizing returns.

I. Market Analysis:

- **Local Market Dynamics**: Conducting thorough market analysis involves assessing local market conditions, including supply and demand dynamics, economic indicators, demographic trends, and regulatory factors. Understanding the nuances of the local market is crucial for identifying investment opportunities and mitigating risks.

- **Property Valuation**: Market analysis informs property valuation by providing insights into comparable sales, rental rates, and property appreciation trends. By analyzing recent transactions and market data, investors can accurately assess the value of potential investment properties and negotiate favorable purchase prices.

- **Risk Assessment**: Market analysis enables investors to identify and assess various risks associated with real estate investment, such as market volatility, economic downturns, and regulatory changes. By conducting comprehensive risk assessments, investors can implement strategies to mitigate risks and safeguard their investment portfolios.

II. Emerging Trends:

- **Technology Integration**: The real estate industry is experiencing a rapid transformation driven by technological advancements. Emerging trends such as virtual property tours, online property marketplaces, and predictive analytics are reshaping how properties are bought, sold, and managed. Investors who embrace technology can gain a competitive edge and capitalize on new opportunities in the market.

- **Sustainable Investing**: Environmental, social, and governance (ESG) considerations are becoming increasingly important in real estate investment decision-making. Sustainable investing practices, such as energy-efficient building design, green certifications, and socially responsible property management, are gaining traction among investors seeking to align their investment portfolios with sustainability goals and societal values.

- **Shifts in Consumer Preferences**: Changing consumer preferences, driven by demographic shifts and lifestyle trends, influence demand for different types of real estate assets. Trends such as urbanization, remote work, and mixed-use developments are shaping the future of real estate investment. Investors who anticipate and adapt to these shifts can capitalize on emerging opportunities and maximize investment returns.

III. Economic Indicators:

- **Employment Trends**: Employment data, including job growth, unemployment rates, and wage growth, are key indicators of local market health and demand for real estate. Strong job markets attract residents and businesses, driving demand for housing and commercial space.
- **Interest Rates**: Interest rates impact borrowing costs and affordability, affecting demand for real estate financing and property sales.

Monitoring interest rate trends and Federal Reserve policies can help investors anticipate market shifts and adjust investment strategies accordingly.

- **Economic Growth**: Overall economic growth indicators, such as GDP growth, consumer spending, and business investment, influence market sentiment and investor confidence. Real estate markets tend to thrive in periods of economic expansion, presenting opportunities for capital appreciation and income generation.

In summary, market analysis and trends play a critical role in real estate investment decision-making. By conducting thorough market research, staying informed about emerging trends, and monitoring key economic indicators, investors can identify lucrative opportunities, mitigate risks, and optimize their investment strategies for success in dynamic real estate markets.

CHAPTER 2:

Setting Investment Goals

Setting clear investment goals is the foundation of a successful investment strategy. Whether aiming for wealth accumulation, retirement planning, or passive income generation, defining specific, measurable, achievable, relevant, and time-bound (SMART) goals provides direction and focus. Investors should consider factors such as risk tolerance, time horizon, and financial objectives when setting goals. Regular review and adjustment of goals ensure alignment with evolving priorities and market conditions, maximizing the likelihood of investment success.

2.1 Defining Investment Objectives

Before embarking on any investment journey, it's crucial to establish clear and concise investment objectives. In this section, we delve into the importance of defining investment objectives and provide guidance on how to articulate goals that align with your financial aspirations.

I. Understanding Investment Objectives:

- **Financial Goals**: Investment objectives serve as the foundation for your investment strategy and guide decision-making processes. Begin by identifying your financial goals, whether they involve wealth accumulation, retirement planning, income generation, or capital preservation. Clarifying your objectives allows you to prioritize investment opportunities and allocate resources effectively.

- **Risk Tolerance**: Consider your risk tolerance when defining investment objectives. Are you comfortable with the potential volatility and fluctuations associated with certain investment strategies, or do you prefer more conservative approaches? Understanding your risk tolerance helps tailor your investment objectives to align with your comfort level and temperament as an investor.

- **Time Horizon**: Your investment time horizon—whether short-term, medium-term, or long-term—greatly influences your investment objectives. Short-term objectives may focus on capital preservation or generating immediate income, while long-term objectives may prioritize wealth accumulation and retirement planning. Aligning your investment objectives with your time horizon ensures a strategic and disciplined approach to achieving your financial goals.

II. Articulating Investment Objectives:

- **Specificity**: Investment objectives should be specific, measurable, achievable, relevant, and time-bound (SMART). Clearly define the desired outcomes, such as target returns, investment timelines, and risk parameters. Avoid vague or ambiguous goals, as they may lead to uncertainty and ineffective decision-making.

- **Flexibility**: Maintain flexibility in your investment objectives to adapt to changing market conditions, personal circumstances, and financial priorities. While it's essential to set clear goals, be open to revising and adjusting them as needed to accommodate evolving investment strategies and market dynamics.

- **Alignment with Values**: Consider aligning your investment objectives with your values and beliefs. Sustainable investing, impact investing, and socially responsible investing are approaches that integrate environmental, social, and governance (ESG) considerations into investment decision-making. By incorporating your values into your investment objectives, you can achieve financial success while making a positive impact on society and the environment.

III. Review and Monitoring:

- **Regular Evaluation**: Periodically review and evaluate your investment objectives to ensure they remain relevant and aligned with your evolving financial situation and goals. Life events, market shifts, and changes in personal circumstances may necessitate adjustments to your investment objectives to stay on track towards achieving your financial aspirations.

- **Monitoring Progress**: Continuously monitor your investment portfolio's performance relative to your investment objectives. Assess whether you're making progress towards achieving your goals and identify any areas that require attention or recalibration. Monitoring progress allows you to course-correct as needed and optimize your investment strategy for success.

- **Seeking Professional Guidance**: Consider seeking professional guidance from financial advisors, investment professionals, or wealth managers to help define, refine, and implement your investment objectives. Experienced professionals can provide valuable insights, strategic recommendations, and personalized guidance tailored to your unique financial situation and goals.

In conclusion, defining investment objectives is a crucial first step in the investment process. By articulating clear, specific, and achievable goals that align with your financial aspirations, risk tolerance, and time horizon, you can establish a solid foundation for building wealth, achieving financial security, and realizing your long-term financial goals.

2.2 Risk Assessment and Management

Effective risk assessment and management are essential components of successful real estate investment strategies. In this section, we delve into the importance of identifying, evaluating, and mitigating risks associated with real estate investments to safeguard capital and optimize returns.

I. Understanding Risk in Real Estate Investment:

- **Types of Risks**: Real estate investment entails various types of risks, including market risk, credit risk, liquidity risk, operational risk, and regulatory risk.

- **Risk-Return Tradeoff**: Investors must understand the risk-return tradeoff inherent in investment decisions and align their investment strategies with their risk preferences.

II. Risk Assessment Strategies:

- **Due Diligence**: Thorough due diligence is essential for assessing and mitigating risks associated with real estate investments. Engage qualified professionals to assist in the due diligence process and provide valuable insights.

- **Financial Analysis**: Perform comprehensive financial analysis to assess potential risks and returns, stress-testing assumptions under various scenarios.

III. Risk Management Strategies:

- **Diversification**: Spread investment capital across different asset classes, geographic locations, and property types to mitigate concentration risk.
- **Insurance Coverage**: Obtain adequate insurance coverage to protect against property damage, liability claims, and other unforeseen events.
- **Reserve Funds**: Establish reserve funds or contingency reserves to

cover unexpected expenses and
ensure liquidity and financial stability.

IV. Continuous Monitoring and Adjustment:

- **Regular Review**: Continuously
  monitor investment portfolios to
  assess performance, identify
  emerging risks, and adjust
  investment strategies accordingly.
- **Adaptability**: Remain adaptable and
  responsive to changing market
  conditions and risk factors, adjusting
  strategies as needed to optimize
  investment returns.

In summary, effective risk assessment and
management are essential for navigating

the complexities of real estate investment and achieving long-term success. By understanding the types of risks inherent in real estate investments, implementing robust risk assessment strategies, and adopting proactive risk management measures, investors can mitigate potential losses, capitalize on opportunities, and achieve their investment objectives with confidence.

2.3 Creating a Realistic Investment Plan

Crafting a realistic investment plan is essential for setting clear objectives, defining strategies, and achieving success in real estate investment. In this section, we explore the key components of creating an effective investment plan tailored to your financial goals, risk tolerance, and investment preferences.

Setting Clear Investment Objectives:

- **Identify Financial Goals**: Begin by identifying your financial goals, whether they involve wealth accumulation, retirement planning, income generation, or capital preservation. Clarifying your objectives allows you to prioritize investment opportunities and allocate resources effectively.

- **Define Risk Tolerance**: Consider your risk tolerance when setting investment objectives. Assess your comfort level with market volatility and fluctuations to align your investment plan with your risk preferences.

Developing a Strategic Investment Strategy:

- **Asset Allocation**: Determine the appropriate asset allocation strategy based on your investment objectives, risk tolerance, and time horizon. Allocate capital across different asset classes, such as stocks, bonds, and real estate, to achieve diversification and manage risk effectively.

- **Property Selection Criteria**: Establish criteria for selecting investment properties, considering factors such as location, property type, market trends, rental potential, and growth prospects. Conduct thorough due diligence to identify properties that align with your investment goals and risk parameters.

Financial Planning and Analysis:

- **Budgeting and Cash Flow Analysis**: Develop a comprehensive budgeting plan to assess your financial resources, expenses, and cash flow projections. Analyze potential investment returns, expenses, and financing options to ensure financial feasibility and sustainability.

- **Risk Management Strategies**: Integrate risk management strategies into your investment plan to mitigate potential risks and preserve capital. Consider insurance coverage, reserve funds, and diversification strategies to safeguard against unexpected events and market fluctuations.

Implementation and Execution:

- **Execution Timeline**: Establish a timeline for implementing your investment plan, outlining specific milestones, deadlines, and action steps. Monitor progress regularly and adjust timelines as needed to stay on track towards achieving your investment goals.

- **Professional Guidance**: Consider seeking professional guidance from financial advisors, real estate professionals, or investment consultants to assist in the implementation and execution of your investment plan. Experienced professionals can provide valuable insights, strategic recommendations, and personalized guidance tailored to your unique financial situation and goals.

Regular Review and Adjustment:

- **Ongoing Monitoring**: Continuously monitor your investment portfolio's performance, market developments, and economic trends to assess progress and identify opportunities for optimization. Regular reviews allow you to stay informed and proactive in managing your investments effectively.

- **Flexibility and Adaptability**: Remain flexible and adaptable in adjusting your investment plan to accommodate changing market conditions, personal circumstances, and financial priorities. Be open to revising strategies, reallocating resources, and exploring new opportunities to optimize investment returns and achieve long-term success.

In summary, creating a realistic investment plan is essential for achieving your financial goals and maximizing returns in real estate investment. By setting clear objectives, developing strategic investment strategies, conducting thorough financial analysis, implementing risk management measures, and regularly reviewing and adjusting your plan, you can navigate the complexities of real estate investment with confidence and achieve sustainable long-term success.

2.4 Long-term vs, Short-term Strategies

Choosing between long-term and short-term strategies is a pivotal decision in real estate investment, each offering distinct advantages and considerations. In this section, we explore the characteristics, benefits, and considerations of both long-term and short-term investment strategies to help investors make informed decisions aligned with their financial goals and risk tolerance.

Long-term Investment Strategies:

- **Wealth Accumulation**: Long-term investment strategies focus on wealth accumulation and capital appreciation over an extended period. Investors adopt a buy-and-hold approach, aiming to benefit from property value appreciation, rental income growth, and long-term market trends.

- **Stability and Predictability**: Long-term investments offer stability and predictability, providing a reliable source of passive income and steady cash flow over time. Rental properties, commercial real estate, and income-producing assets are common long-term investment options favored by investors seeking sustainable returns and portfolio stability.

- **Tax Efficiency**: Long-term investments may offer tax advantages, including favorable capital gains treatment, depreciation deductions, and tax deferral opportunities. By holding investments for an extended period, investors may benefit from preferential tax treatment and maximize after-tax returns.

Short-term Investment Strategies:

- **Capital Growth**: Short-term investment strategies prioritize capital growth and quick returns within a relatively brief investment horizon. Investors focus on opportunistic investments, such as fix-and-flip properties, distressed assets, or value-added opportunities, aiming to capitalize on market inefficiencies and short-term market trends.

- **Liquidity and Flexibility**: Short-term investments offer liquidity and flexibility, allowing investors to capitalize on immediate market opportunities and adapt to changing market conditions. Investors can enter and exit investments quickly, leveraging market timing and agility to maximize returns and minimize exposure to long-term market risks.

- **Risk and Volatility**: Short-term investments entail higher risk and volatility compared to long-term strategies, as they are more susceptible to market fluctuations, economic cycles, and unforeseen events. Investors must carefully assess risk-reward dynamics and implement risk management strategies to mitigate potential losses and preserve capital.

Considerations for Choosing Strategies:

- **Investment Objectives**: Align your investment strategy with your financial goals, risk tolerance, and time horizon. Long-term strategies may be suitable for wealth accumulation and retirement planning, while short-term strategies may be better suited for capital growth and opportunistic investing.

- **Market Conditions**: Consider prevailing market conditions, economic trends, and interest rate environments when selecting investment strategies. Long-term strategies may be favorable in stable or appreciating markets, while short-term strategies may thrive in dynamic or transitional market environments.

Risk Management: Implement robust risk management measures regardless of the chosen investment strategy. Diversification, due diligence, insurance coverage, and contingency planning are essential for mitigating risks and safeguarding investments against unforeseen events.

In summary, the choice between long-term and short-term investment strategies depends on individual preferences, financial objectives, and market conditions. Long-term strategies offer stability, predictability, and tax advantages, while short-term strategies provide liquidity, flexibility, and potential for quick returns. By understanding the characteristics, benefits, and considerations of each strategy, investors can develop a balanced and diversified investment portfolio tailored to their unique financial goals and risk tolerance.

CHAPTER 3:

Financial Fundamentals

Understanding financial fundamentals is essential for effective investment management. It involves mastering concepts such as budgeting, saving, investing, and debt management. By establishing a solid financial foundation, individuals can make informed decisions, optimize wealth accumulation, and achieve their long-term financial goals. Key principles include living within means, diversifying investments, managing risk, and maintaining a disciplined approach to financial planning. With a grasp of financial fundamentals, individuals can navigate economic uncertainties and build a secure financial future.

3.1 Understanding Real Estate Financing

Comprehending real estate financing is crucial for successful investment ventures. In this section, we explore the fundamentals of real estate financing, including various financing options, terms, and considerations to help investors make informed decisions and optimize their investment strategies.

Types of Real Estate Financing:

- **Traditional Mortgage Loans**: Traditional mortgage loans are the most common form of real estate financing, offering fixed or adjustable interest rates and terms ranging from

15 to 30 years. Borrowers provide a down payment and repay the loan, typically with monthly installments, until the loan is fully amortized.

- Commercial Loans: Commercial loans are tailored for financing commercial real estate properties such as office buildings, retail centers, and industrial warehouses. These loans may feature different terms, interest rates, and underwriting criteria compared to residential mortgage loans.

- **Government-Backed Loans**: Government-backed loans, including FHA loans, VA loans, and USDA loans, are insured or guaranteed by government agencies, making them accessible to borrowers with lower credit scores or smaller down payments. These loans often offer competitive terms and favorable interest rates.

- **Private Financing**: Private financing involves borrowing from private lenders, individuals, or investment groups instead of traditional financial institutions. Private financing may offer flexibility, speed, and unique terms tailored to individual borrower needs but may come with higher interest rates and fees.

Financing Considerations:

- **Down Payment**: The down payment is a percentage of the property's purchase price paid upfront by the borrower. The size of the down payment affects loan eligibility, interest rates, and overall financing costs. Higher down payments may result in lower loan-to-value ratios and better loan terms.

- **Interest Rates**: Interest rates determine the cost of borrowing and impact monthly mortgage payments. Fixed-rate mortgages offer stability and predictability, while adjustable-rate mortgages (ARMs) may offer lower initial rates but carry the risk of rate fluctuations over time.

- **Loan Terms**: Loan terms, including repayment period, amortization schedule, and prepayment penalties, vary depending on the type of loan and lender. Longer loan terms may result in lower monthly payments but higher total interest costs over the life of the loan.

Qualifying for Financing:

- **Credit Score**: Credit score is a critical factor in loan qualification and determines the borrower's creditworthiness. Lenders use credit scores to assess the risk of default and may offer better loan terms to borrowers with higher credit scores.

- **Debt-to-Income Ratio**: Debt-to-income (DTI) ratio measures the borrower's monthly debt obligations relative to their income.

Lenders use DTI ratios to evaluate the borrower's ability to repay the loan and may require lower DTI ratios for loan approval.

- **Documentation Requirements**: Borrowers must provide various documentation, including income verification, asset statements, tax returns, and employment history, to qualify for financing. Meeting documentation requirements is essential for loan approval and securing favorable financing terms.

Risk Management Strategies:

- **Appraisal and Due Diligence**: Conducting thorough property appraisals and due diligence is essential for assessing property value, market trends, and potential risks. Appraisals provide an objective assessment of the property's worth, ensuring that borrowers do not overpay or encounter financing challenges.

- **Contingency Planning**: Implement contingency plans to mitigate financing risks and address unforeseen challenges. Contingency funds, alternative financing options, and exit strategies can help borrowers navigate financing obstacles and safeguard investment projects.

In summary, understanding real estate financing is essential for navigating the complexities of real estate investment and maximizing investment returns. By exploring various financing options, terms, and considerations, investors can make informed decisions, secure favorable financing terms, and optimize their investment strategies for success in dynamic real estate markets.

3.2 Mortgage Options and Considerations

Mortgages play a pivotal role in real estate investment, offering financing solutions tailored to individual needs and preferences. In this section, we explore different mortgage options, terms, and considerations to help investors navigate the mortgage landscape effectively and optimize their investment strategies.

1. Types of Mortgages:

- **Fixed-Rate Mortgages**: Fixed-rate mortgages feature a stable interest rate and consistent monthly payments throughout the loan term. This type of mortgage provides predictability and protection against interest rate fluctuations, making it ideal for investors seeking long-term stability and budgeting certainty.

- **Adjustable-Rate Mortgages (ARMs)**: ARMs offer an initial fixed interest rate period followed by adjustable rates that fluctuate based on market conditions. While ARMs may offer lower initial interest rates and payments, they carry the risk of rate increases over time, potentially leading to higher payments and increased financing costs.

- **Interest-Only Mortgages**: Interest-only mortgages allow borrowers to pay only the interest portion of the loan for a specified period, typically ranging from five to ten years. After the interest-only period expires, borrowers must repay both principal and interest, resulting in higher monthly payments. Interest-only mortgages may appeal to investors seeking flexibility and lower initial payments but require careful planning for future payment increases.

2. Mortgage Terms and Features:

- **Loan Term**: Mortgage terms vary in length, typically ranging from 15 to 30 years. Shorter loan terms result in higher monthly payments but lower total interest costs over the life of the loan, while longer loan terms offer lower monthly payments but higher overall interest expenses.

- **Down Payment Requirements**: Down payment requirements vary depending on the type of mortgage, loan amount, and borrower qualifications. Conventional mortgages typically require down payments ranging from 3% to 20% of the property's purchase price, while government-backed loans may offer lower down payment options for eligible borrowers.

- **Private Mortgage Insurance (PMI)**: Borrowers who make a down payment of less than 20% of the property's purchase price may be required to pay private mortgage insurance (PMI) to protect the lender against default. PMI adds to the borrower's monthly mortgage payments and increases the overall cost of financing.

3. Considerations for Mortgage Selection:

- **Financial Goals and Risk Tolerance**: Consider your financial goals, risk tolerance, and long-term investment objectives when selecting a mortgage. Fixed-rate mortgages offer stability and predictability, while ARMs may provide lower initial payments but carry the risk of rate fluctuations.

- **Budget and Cash Flow**: Evaluate your budget and cash flow to determine affordability and suitability of mortgage options. Calculate monthly mortgage payments, including principal, interest, taxes, insurance, and potential PMI, to ensure they align with your financial capabilities and investment goals.

- **Market Conditions and Economic Outlook**: Monitor market conditions, economic trends, and interest rate forecasts when selecting a mortgage. Assess potential impacts of interest rate changes on mortgage payments and overall financing costs, and consider locking in favorable rates when appropriate.

4. Mortgage Pre-Approval and Documentation:

- **Pre-Approval Process**: Obtain mortgage pre-approval to assess loan eligibility, determine borrowing capacity, and demonstrate financial readiness to sellers. Pre-approval involves submitting documentation, such as income verification, asset statements, and credit history, to lenders for evaluation.

- **Documentation Requirements**: Prepare necessary documentation, including income verification, tax returns, bank statements, and employment history, for the mortgage application process. Meeting documentation requirements and providing accurate information are essential for securing mortgage approval and favorable financing terms.

In summary, understanding mortgage options and considerations is crucial for real estate investors seeking financing for their investment properties. By exploring different mortgage types, terms, and features, investors can select mortgage solutions that align with their financial goals, risk tolerance, and investment strategies, ultimately optimizing their real estate investment endeavors.

3.3 Evaluating Return on Investment (ROI)

Assessing the return on investment (ROI) is essential for real estate investors to gauge the profitability and performance of their investment ventures. In this section, we delve into the key metrics, methodologies, and considerations for evaluating ROI in real estate investment to make informed decisions and optimize investment outcomes.

1. Understanding Return on Investment (ROI):

- **Definition**: ROI measures the profitability of an investment relative to its cost, expressed as a percentage. It evaluates the efficiency of capital deployment and quantifies the return generated from the investment relative to the initial investment amount.

- **Components**: ROI considers both the gains generated from the investment, such as rental income, appreciation, and tax benefits, as well as the costs associated with acquiring, operating, and maintaining the investment property.

2. Key Metrics for Evaluating ROI:

- **Cash-on-Cash Return**: Cash-on-cash return calculates the annual return generated from the investment relative to the initial cash investment. It provides a straightforward measure of cash flow efficiency and is calculated by dividing the annual net operating income (NOI) by the initial cash investment.

- **Cap Rate (Capitalization Rate)**: Cap rate measures the relationship between the net operating income (NOI) generated by the property and its market value. It serves as a benchmark for comparing investment opportunities and is calculated by dividing the property's NOI by its market value or purchase price.

- **Internal Rate of Return (IRR)**: IRR represents the annualized rate of return generated by the investment over its holding period, accounting for both cash flows and the time value of money. It accounts for the timing and magnitude of cash flows and provides a comprehensive measure of investment performance.

3. Methodologies for ROI Analysis:

- **Comparative Analysis**: Conduct comparative analysis to benchmark ROI metrics against similar properties, market averages, or industry standards. Comparative analysis provides context and insights into the relative performance of the investment and helps identify opportunities for improvement.
- **Sensitivity Analysis**: Perform sensitivity analysis to assess the impact of changing market conditions, assumptions, or variables on ROI metrics. Sensitivity analysis

helps investors understand the risk-reward dynamics of the investment and make informed decisions under different scenarios.

4. Considerations for Evaluating ROI:

- **Risk Assessment**: Consider the inherent risks and uncertainties associated with real estate investment when evaluating ROI. Assess factors such as market volatility, economic trends, vacancy rates, and regulatory changes to gauge investment risk and adjust ROI expectations accordingly.

- **Long-Term Perspective**: Take a long-term perspective when evaluating ROI to account for potential appreciation, equity buildup, and tax benefits over the investment horizon. Long-term investment strategies may yield higher overall returns but require patience and strategic planning.

5. Continuous Monitoring and Optimization:

- **Regular Review**: Continuously monitor ROI metrics and performance indicators to assess investment progress and identify opportunities for optimization. Regular reviews allow investors to make proactive adjustments, optimize cash flow, and enhance overall investment returns.

- **Portfolio Diversification**: Diversify investment portfolios across different asset classes, geographic locations, and property types to mitigate risk and optimize overall ROI. Diversification spreads risk and maximizes opportunities for generating consistent returns across diverse market conditions.

In summary, evaluating return on investment (ROI) is essential for real estate investors to assess the profitability and performance of their investment ventures effectively. By understanding key metrics, methodologies, and considerations for ROI analysis, investors can make informed decisions, optimize investment outcomes, and achieve long-term success in real estate markets.

3.4 Tax Implications and Strategies

Understanding the tax implications of real estate investment is essential for maximizing returns and optimizing tax efficiency. In this section, we explore key tax considerations, strategies, and incentives to help investors navigate the complex landscape of real estate taxation and enhance their investment outcomes.

1. Tax Implications of Real Estate Investment:

- **Rental Income Taxation**: Rental income generated from investment properties is subject to federal and state income taxes. Rental income is generally taxed at the taxpayer's marginal income tax rate, with deductions allowed for rental expenses, depreciation, and other eligible deductions.

- **Capital Gains Tax**: Profits from the sale of investment properties are subject to capital gains tax. Short-term capital gains, generated from properties held for less than one year, are taxed at ordinary income tax rates, while long-term capital gains, from properties held for more than one year, are taxed at preferential capital gains tax rates.

- **Depreciation Deductions**: Real estate investors can claim depreciation deductions on investment properties to recover the cost of acquiring and improving the property over its useful life. Depreciation deductions reduce taxable income and provide valuable tax savings for investors.

2. Tax Planning Strategies for Real Estate Investors:

- **1031 Exchange**: Utilize a 1031 exchange, also known as a like-kind exchange, to defer capital gains taxes on the sale of investment properties by reinvesting proceeds into similar properties. 1031 exchanges allow investors to defer taxes indefinitely, providing opportunities for portfolio growth and tax deferral.

- **Qualified Opportunity Zones (QOZs)**: Invest in designated Qualified Opportunity Zones to take advantage of tax incentives, including deferral and reduction of capital gains taxes. Qualified Opportunity Funds allow investors to defer capital gains taxes by reinvesting gains into designated economically distressed areas.

- **Strategic Asset Allocation**: Implement strategic asset allocation strategies to optimize tax efficiency and minimize tax liabilities. Consider holding properties in tax-advantaged accounts, such as self-directed IRAs or 401(k) plans, to benefit from tax-deferred growth and potential tax savings.

3. Tax Deductions and Credits:

- **Mortgage Interest Deduction**: Deduct mortgage interest payments on investment properties as an allowable expense, reducing taxable rental income and lowering overall tax liabilities. Mortgage interest deductions can provide significant tax savings for real estate investors.

- **Property Tax Deduction**: Deduct property taxes paid on investment properties as allowable expenses, reducing taxable rental income and providing additional tax savings for investors. Property tax deductions help offset operating expenses and improve cash flow for investment properties.

- **Pass-Through Deductions**: Take advantage of pass-through deductions available to real estate investors who operate as sole proprietors, partnerships, or pass-through entities. Qualified business income deductions allow eligible taxpayers to deduct up to 20% of qualified real estate income,

reducing taxable income and
providing valuable tax savings.

4. Consultation and Professional Guidance:

- **Tax Advisors and Accountants**:
  Consult experienced tax advisors,
  accountants, and tax professionals
  specializing in real estate taxation to
  develop tailored tax strategies and
  maximize tax efficiency. Experienced
  professionals can provide valuable
  insights, strategic recommendations,
  and personalized guidance to
  optimize tax outcomes and enhance
  investment returns.

- **Continued Education**: Stay
  informed about changes in tax laws,

regulations, and incentives affecting real estate investment. Continued education and awareness of tax planning opportunities allow investors to adapt strategies, leverage incentives, and optimize tax outcomes for their investment portfolios.

In summary, understanding tax implications and implementing tax planning strategies are essential components of successful real estate investment. By considering key tax considerations, leveraging tax incentives, and consulting with qualified tax professionals, investors can optimize tax efficiency, minimize tax liabilities, and enhance overall investment outcomes in real estate markets.

CHAPTER 4:

Property Selection and Due Diligence

Selecting the right property and conducting thorough due diligence are critical steps in real estate investment. Property selection involves identifying properties that align with your investment goals, risk tolerance, and financial objectives. Factors such as location, property type, market trends, rental potential, and growth prospects play a crucial role in determining the suitability of a property for investment.

Once a property of interest is identified, due diligence becomes paramount. Due diligence involves conducting comprehensive research and analysis to assess the property's condition, value, and investment potential. This process may include reviewing financial documents, conducting property inspections, evaluating market comparables, and assessing legal and regulatory compliance.

By carefully selecting properties and performing diligent due diligence, investors can mitigate risks, identify opportunities, and make informed investment decisions. Successful property selection and due diligence lay the foundation for profitable real estate investments and contribute to long-term investment success.

4.1 Location Analysis and Factors to Consider

Location analysis is a critical aspect of real estate investment, as it directly impacts property value, rental potential, and long-term appreciation. In this section, we explore the key factors to consider when evaluating locations for investment properties to make informed decisions and maximize investment returns.

1. Accessibility and Convenience:

- **Transportation Infrastructure**: Assess the accessibility of the location in terms of highways, public transportation, and proximity to airports. Properties located near major transportation hubs or with easy access to highways tend to attract tenants and command higher rental rates.

- **Amenities and Services**: Consider the availability of essential amenities and services such as schools, healthcare facilities, shopping centers, restaurants, and recreational areas. Properties situated in neighborhoods with convenient

access to amenities are more
desirable to tenants and potential
buyers.

2. Economic and Job Growth:

- **Employment Opportunities**:
  Evaluate the local job market and
  economic indicators to gauge
  employment growth and stability.
  Investing in locations with diverse
  industries, strong job growth, and low
  unemployment rates can lead to
  higher demand for rental properties
  and increased property values.
- **Business Development**: Monitor
  business developments, corporate
  relocations, and infrastructure
  projects in the area. Locations

experiencing economic expansion, new business investments, and urban revitalization efforts often present lucrative investment opportunities.

3. Market Dynamics and Demand:

Supply and Demand: Analyze supply and demand dynamics in the local real estate market to assess market equilibrium and rental demand. Investing in areas with limited housing supply and high demand from tenants can lead to competitive rental yields and property appreciation.

- **Population Trends**: Consider population growth rates, demographic trends, and household formations in the area. Properties located in regions experiencing population growth, urbanization, and influx of young professionals or retirees tend to experience strong demand and appreciation.

4. Neighborhood Quality and Safety:

- **Crime Rates**: Research crime statistics and safety ratings to evaluate the overall safety and security of the neighborhood. Properties located in low-crime areas with well-maintained streets, parks, and public spaces are more attractive to tenants and command higher property values.

- **School Districts**: Assess the quality of local school districts and educational institutions, as it can influence property values and rental demand. Properties located in neighborhoods with top-rated schools and access to quality education often appeal to families and attract long-term tenants.

5. Regulatory Environment and Development:

- **Zoning and Regulations**: Familiarize yourself with local zoning regulations, land use policies, and development restrictions. Understanding zoning ordinances and regulatory requirements is essential for assessing development potential, property use limitations, and future growth prospects.

- **Development Plans**: Stay informed about municipal development plans, infrastructure projects, and urban redevelopment initiatives in the area. Properties located in neighborhoods undergoing gentrification, revitalization, or urban renewal efforts may experience accelerated appreciation and investment returns.

In summary, location analysis is a fundamental aspect of real estate investment, influencing property performance and investment outcomes. By considering factors such as accessibility, economic growth, market dynamics, neighborhood quality, and regulatory environment, investors can identify prime locations, mitigate risks, and capitalize on lucrative investment opportunities in dynamic real estate markets.

4.2 Property Types and Market Demand

Understanding property types and market demand is essential for real estate investors to identify profitable investment opportunities and meet the needs of potential tenants or buyers. In this section, we explore the various types of properties and analyze market demand factors to guide investment decisions effectively.

1. Residential Properties:

- **Single-Family Homes**: Single-family homes are standalone properties designed to accommodate one family or household. They appeal to tenants seeking privacy, space, and a sense of ownership. Market demand for single-family homes varies based on factors such as location, affordability, and lifestyle preferences.

- **Multi-Family Properties**: Multi-family properties, including duplexes, triplexes, and apartment buildings, consist of multiple residential units within a single structure. They offer rental income potential and economies of scale for investors. Market demand for multi-family properties is influenced by rental affordability, population growth, and housing preferences.

2. Commercial Properties:

- **Office Buildings**: Office buildings provide office space for businesses, professional services, and commercial tenants. Market demand for office space is driven by factors such as economic growth, employment trends, and business expansion. Location, accessibility, and amenities are key considerations for tenants seeking office space.

- **Retail Centers**: Retail centers comprise shopping malls, strip malls, and retail outlets offering space for retail stores, restaurants, and service providers. Market demand for retail space depends on consumer spending, population demographics, and foot traffic. High-traffic locations with strong demographics attract retailers and command higher rents.

3. Industrial Properties:

- **Warehouse and Distribution Centers**: Warehouse and distribution centers are facilities used for storage, logistics, and distribution of goods and merchandise. Market demand for industrial properties is driven by e-commerce growth, supply chain logistics, and manufacturing activity. Proximity to transportation hubs and access to major highways are critical factors for industrial tenants.

- **Flex Space**: Flex space properties offer versatile space for a combination of office, warehouse, and light manufacturing purposes. Market demand for flex space is influenced by small businesses, startups, and technology companies seeking flexible workspace solutions. Location, accessibility, and customization options are key considerations for tenants.

4. Specialized Properties:

- **Hospitality Properties**: Hospitality properties include hotels, motels, and short-term rental accommodations catering to travelers and tourists. Market demand for hospitality properties fluctuates based on tourism trends, travel patterns, and economic conditions. Location, amenities, and guest experience are critical factors for hospitality investors.

- **Healthcare Properties**: Healthcare properties encompass medical office buildings, clinics, and specialized facilities serving the healthcare industry. Market demand for healthcare properties is driven by population demographics, healthcare services demand, and proximity to medical facilities. Location, accessibility, and healthcare infrastructure are key considerations for healthcare investors.

5. Mixed-Use Developments:

- **Mixed-Use Properties**: Mixed-use developments combine residential, commercial, and retail components within a single project. Market demand for mixed-use properties stems from urban lifestyle preferences, walkability, and convenience. Mixed-use developments create vibrant communities, offering residents and tenants access to diverse amenities and services.

In summary, understanding property types and market demand is crucial for real estate investors to identify lucrative investment opportunities and align with tenant or buyer preferences. By analyzing factors such as property usage, location, demographics, and economic trends, investors can make informed decisions and capitalize on emerging trends in dynamic real estate markets.

4.3 Conducting Due Diligence

Conducting due diligence is a critical step in real estate investment to assess the viability, risks, and potential returns of a property. In this section, we explore the key components and best practices for conducting thorough due diligence to make informed investment decisions and mitigate risks effectively.

1. Financial Analysis:

- **Income and Expenses**: Review the property's income and expense statements to assess its financial performance. Analyze rental income, operating expenses, vacancy rates, and potential capital expenditures to determine cash flow projections and investment viability.

- **Financial Projections**: Develop financial projections based on market rents, occupancy rates, and operating expenses to evaluate investment returns and cash flow potential. Consider factors such as rental market trends, inflation rates, and economic conditions when forecasting future performance.

2. Property Inspection:

- **Physical Condition**: Conduct a comprehensive property inspection to assess its physical condition, structural integrity, and maintenance needs. Identify any existing issues or potential hazards, such as structural defects, roof damage, plumbing issues, or environmental hazards, that may require remediation.

- **Code Compliance**: Verify that the property complies with building codes, zoning regulations, and safety standards. Assess any outstanding permits, violations, or compliance issues that may affect property value, occupancy, or resale potential.

3. Legal and Title Review:

- **Title Search**: Conduct a title search to verify ownership, liens, encumbrances, and easements affecting the property. Confirm clear and marketable title ownership to avoid legal disputes or title defects that may impede the sale or financing of the property.

- **Legal Documents**: Review legal documents such as purchase agreements, leases, property deeds, and condominium documents to understand rights, obligations, and restrictions associated with the property. Consult legal professionals to clarify legal terms, resolve ambiguities, and ensure compliance with contractual obligations.

4. Market Analysis:

- **Market Trends**: Analyze local market trends, comparable sales, and rental comparables to assess property value, rental rates, and market demand. Consider factors such as supply and demand dynamics, demographic trends, and economic indicators influencing the local real estate market.

- **Competitive Analysis**: Evaluate competing properties in the area to benchmark pricing, amenities, and market positioning. Identify competitive advantages, market niches, and opportunities to differentiate the property and attract tenants or buyers effectively.

5. Environmental and Regulatory Considerations:

- **Environmental Assessment**:
  Conduct environmental
  assessments, including Phase I
  environmental site assessments
  (ESAs), to identify potential
  environmental risks or contamination
  on the property. Address any
  environmental concerns and
  compliance issues to mitigate liability
  and ensure regulatory compliance.
- **Regulatory Review**: Review zoning
  ordinances, land use regulations,
  and planning documents to
  understand development restrictions,
  allowable uses, and future
  development potential. Assess any
  regulatory constraints or rezoning

proposals that may impact property value or development opportunities.

In summary, conducting due diligence is essential for real estate investors to evaluate the financial, physical, legal, and market aspects of a property thoroughly. By performing comprehensive analysis, inspections, and reviews, investors can identify risks, uncover opportunities, and make informed investment decisions that align with their investment objectives and risk tolerance.

4.4 Assessing Property Value and Potential

Assessing property value and potential is crucial for real estate investors to make informed decisions and maximize returns on their investments. In this section, we explore the key methodologies, factors, and considerations for evaluating property value and unlocking its potential for profitability.

1. Comparative Market Analysis (CMA):

- **Comparable Sales**: Conduct a comparative market analysis (CMA) by analyzing recent sales of similar properties in the area. Compare factors such as property size, location, condition, and amenities to determine the fair market value of the subject property.

- **Market Trends**: Consider market trends, including appreciation rates, supply and demand dynamics, and economic indicators, to assess property value trends and forecast future appreciation potential. Analyze historical sales data and market forecasts to gauge market stability and growth prospects.

2. Income Approach:

- **Capitalization Rate (Cap Rate)**: Use the income approach to value investment properties based on their income-generating potential. Calculate the property's capitalization rate (cap rate) by dividing the net operating income (NOI) by the property's purchase price or market value. Cap rates vary by property type, location, and market conditions, reflecting the property's risk and return profile.

- **Gross Rent Multiplier (GRM)**: Apply the gross rent multiplier (GRM) method to estimate property value based on its gross rental income. Divide the property's purchase price or market value by its gross annual rental income to derive the GRM. GRM provides a quick valuation metric but may oversimplify factors such as expenses and vacancy rates.

3. Cost Approach:

- **Replacement Cost**: Assess property value using the cost approach, which estimates the cost to replace or reproduce the property's improvements at current market prices. Consider factors such as construction costs, depreciation, and obsolescence to determine the property's replacement value.

- **Depreciation Analysis**: Evaluate depreciation factors, including physical, functional, and economic obsolescence, to adjust the property's replacement cost for accrued depreciation. Account for age, condition, maintenance history, and market trends to calculate

depreciation allowances accurately.

4. Value-Add Opportunities:

- **Renovation and Rehabilitation**:
  Identify value-add opportunities to
  increase property value through
  renovation, rehabilitation, or
  redevelopment projects. Assess the
  feasibility, costs, and potential returns
  of property improvements, upgrades,
  or expansions to enhance market
  appeal and rental income potential.

- **Strategic Repositioning**: Explore
  strategic repositioning strategies,
  such as rebranding, repositioning, or
  reimagining the property's use or
  target market. Evaluate market

demand, demographic trends, and competitive positioning to identify opportunities for optimizing property performance and maximizing returns.

5. Risk Assessment and Contingencies:

- **Risk Management**: Assess property-specific risks, including market volatility, economic downturns, tenant turnover, and regulatory changes, to mitigate potential downside risks and protect investment capital. Implement risk management strategies, such as diversification, insurance, and contingency planning, to safeguard against unforeseen events.

- **Contingency Planning**: Develop contingency plans and exit strategies to mitigate risks and adapt to changing market conditions. Establish alternative scenarios, financial buffers, and exit options to minimize losses and capitalize on opportunities as they arise during the investment lifecycle.

In summary, assessing property value and potential requires a comprehensive analysis of market data, income projections, cost considerations, and value-add opportunities. By utilizing various valuation methods, conducting thorough due diligence, and identifying value-enhancement strategies, investors can make informed decisions, optimize investment returns, and unlock the full potential of their real estate investments.

CHAPTER 5:

Negotiation and Acquisition

Negotiation and acquisition are integral components of successful real estate investment. Effective negotiation skills, coupled with strategic acquisition tactics, can help investors secure favorable deals, maximize value, and achieve investment objectives. Key principles include conducting thorough market research, understanding seller motivations, and leveraging information asymmetry to negotiate advantageous terms. By employing strategic negotiation techniques and conducting diligent due diligence, investors can navigate complex transactions, mitigate risks, and capitalize on opportunities to acquire properties that align with their investment goals.

5.1 Negotiation Strategies and Tactics

Negotiation strategies and tactics play a pivotal role in real estate transactions, allowing investors to secure favorable deals, optimize terms, and achieve their investment objectives. In this section, we explore key strategies and tactics for effective negotiation in real estate investment.

1. Preparation and Research:

- **Market Analysis**: Conduct thorough market research and analysis to understand current market trends, comparable sales, and property values. Gather information on the property, seller motivations, and competing offers to inform your negotiation strategy.

- Know Your Goals: Clarify your investment goals, priorities, and desired outcomes before entering negotiations. Establish your maximum purchase price, desired terms, and contingency plans to guide your negotiation strategy effectively.

2. Build Rapport and Trust:

- **Establish Relationships**: Build rapport and trust with the seller or their representatives to foster open communication and cooperation during negotiations. Demonstrate professionalism, integrity, and sincerity to create a positive negotiation environment.

- **Active Listening**: Practice active listening to understand the seller's needs, concerns, and motivations. Ask probing questions, empathize with their perspective, and seek common ground to build trust and rapport throughout the negotiation process.

3. Positioning and Leverage:

- **Positioning**: Position yourself as a serious and qualified buyer by demonstrating financial readiness, credibility, and commitment to the transaction. Present a compelling offer package that highlights your strengths as a buyer, such as pre-approval letters, proof of funds, and flexible terms.

- **Leverage Points**: Identify leverage points and negotiation variables that can be leveraged to your advantage. Factors such as market conditions, property conditions, time constraints, and seller motivations can influence negotiation dynamics and create opportunities for favorable terms.

4. Creative Solutions and Win-Win Outcomes:

- **Problem-Solving Approach**: Adopt a problem-solving mindset and explore creative solutions to address obstacles and challenges during negotiations. Propose win-win solutions that meet the needs of both parties and facilitate mutual agreement on terms.

- **Value Proposition**: Emphasize the value proposition of your offer, highlighting the benefits and advantages for the seller. Showcase your ability to close quickly, provide certainty of transaction, and offer favorable terms to incentivize acceptance of your offer.

5. Negotiation Techniques:

- **Anchoring**: Use anchoring techniques to set a reference point or starting position for negotiations. Present initial offers or terms that anchor the negotiation discussions and influence subsequent counteroffers and concessions.

- **Compromise and Concession**: Practice strategic compromise and concession management to reach mutually acceptable agreements. Prioritize your negotiation objectives, identify non-essential concessions, and trade-off concessions strategically to maintain leverage and achieve your primary goals.

In summary, negotiation strategies and tactics are essential skills for real estate investors to successfully navigate transactions, secure favorable deals, and achieve their investment objectives. By preparing diligently, building rapport, leveraging positioning and leverage, exploring creative solutions, and employing effective negotiation techniques, investors can optimize negotiation outcomes and maximize value in real estate transactions.

5.2 Making Competitive Offers

Crafting competitive offers is essential in real estate investment to stand out in a competitive market, secure desirable properties, and optimize investment opportunities. In this section, we delve into strategies and best practices for making compelling and competitive offers in real estate transactions.

1. Market Analysis and Comparative Pricing:

- **Comparable Sales**: Conduct thorough market research to identify comparable sales (comps) and assess the fair market value of the property. Analyze recent sales data, property characteristics, and market trends to determine competitive pricing and inform your offer strategy.

- **Price Analysis**: Evaluate pricing strategies, such as pricing at or slightly below market value, to attract seller interest and position your offer competitively. Consider factors such as property condition, location, and demand dynamics when determining offer price.

2. Financial Preparations and Pre-Approval:

- **Financial Readiness**: Ensure financial readiness by obtaining pre-approval for mortgage financing or securing proof of funds for cash offers. Demonstrate financial stability, credibility, and readiness to proceed with the transaction to strengthen your offer's appeal to sellers.

- **Offer Terms**: Structure offer terms to reflect financial strength and flexibility, such as offering earnest money deposits, waiving financing contingencies, or providing quick closing timelines. Presenting favorable offer terms can differentiate your offer and increase its competitiveness.

3. Understanding Seller Motivations:

- **Seller Motivations**: Understand seller motivations, goals, and circumstances to tailor your offer strategy accordingly. Factors such as time constraints, financial needs, and emotional attachment to the property can influence seller decision-making and acceptance of offers.

- **Personalized Approach**:
  Personalize your offer presentation to
  resonate with seller motivations and
  preferences. Highlight aspects of
  your offer that address seller
  concerns, mitigate risks, and align
  with their objectives to increase the
  likelihood of acceptance.

4. Flexibility and Contingencies:

- **Contingency Planning**: Include
  appropriate contingencies in your
  offer to protect your interests and
  provide flexibility during due
  diligence. Common contingencies
  include inspection contingencies,
  financing contingencies, and
  appraisal contingencies, which allow
  you to renegotiate or withdraw the
  offer if certain conditions are not met.

- **Flexibility**: Demonstrate flexibility in
  negotiation and willingness to
  accommodate seller needs or
  preferences within reason. Adjust
  offer terms, timelines, or

contingencies to address seller concerns and increase the attractiveness of your offer.

5. Timeliness and Communication:

- **Timely Submission**: Submit offers promptly and efficiently to demonstrate seriousness and urgency. Act decisively and capitalize on favorable market opportunities to avoid missing out on desirable properties.

- **Clear Communication**: Communicate clearly and effectively with the seller or their representatives throughout the offer process. Provide complete offer packages, address questions or concerns promptly, and maintain professional communication to facilitate negotiation and decision-making.

In summary, making competitive offers in real estate investment requires a strategic approach, market knowledge, and understanding of seller motivations. By conducting thorough market analysis, preparing financially, tailoring offers to seller preferences, incorporating flexibility and contingencies, and communicating effectively, investors can craft compelling offers that stand out in competitive markets and increase the likelihood of successful transactions.

5.3 Securing Financing and Closing Deals

Securing financing and closing deals are pivotal steps in real estate investment, enabling investors to fund property acquisitions and finalize transactions. In this section, we explore strategies and considerations for securing financing, navigating the closing process, and completing successful real estate transactions.

1. Financial Preparations:

- **Creditworthiness Assessment**: Assess your creditworthiness by reviewing your credit report, credit score, and financial history. Address any discrepancies or issues that may impact your ability to qualify for financing or affect loan terms.

- **Financial Documentation**: Prepare necessary financial documentation, including income statements, tax returns, bank statements, and asset verification documents, to support your loan application. Ensure accuracy, completeness, and transparency in your financial disclosures to facilitate loan approval.

2. Financing Options:

- **Mortgage Financing**: Explore mortgage financing options, including conventional loans, government-backed loans (FHA, VA, USDA), and portfolio loans, to determine the most suitable financing option for your investment property. Compare interest rates, loan terms, and eligibility requirements to select the best financing solution.

- **Alternative Financing**: Consider alternative financing options, such as private lenders, hard money loans, crowdfunding, or seller financing, if traditional mortgage financing is unavailable or restrictive. Evaluate the terms, costs, and risks associated with alternative financing sources before proceeding.

3. Loan Approval Process:

- **Pre-Approval**: Obtain pre-approval for mortgage financing to demonstrate financial readiness and strengthen your offers credibility with sellers. Pre-approval provides a preliminary assessment of your borrowing capacity and streamlines the loan approval process.

- **Underwriting and Due Diligence**: Undergo underwriting and due diligence processes conducted by the lender to assess your creditworthiness, property value, and loan risk. Cooperate with the lender's requests for additional documentation, appraisals, and property inspections to expedite loan approval.

4. Closing Preparation:

- **Closing Costs Estimation**: Estimate closing costs, including loan origination fees, appraisal fees, title insurance, escrow fees, and prepaid expenses, to anticipate total cash outlay required for closing. Budget for closing costs and prepare funds accordingly to avoid last-minute surprises.

- **Title Examination and Insurance**: Conduct title examination and obtain title insurance to verify ownership rights, detect any title defects or encumbrances, and protect against title-related risks. Address any title issues or discrepancies before closing to ensure clear and marketable title transfer.

5. Closing Process:

- **Closing Coordination**: Coordinate closing logistics with the lender, escrow agent, title company, and other parties involved in the transaction. Schedule closing dates, coordinate document signings, and ensure timely completion of all closing requirements to facilitate a smooth and efficient closing process.

- **Closing Documentation**: Review closing documents, including the loan estimate, closing disclosure, promissory note, deed of trust, and settlement statement, carefully before signing. Seek clarification on any terms or conditions, and verify accuracy of information to avoid errors or discrepancies.

6. Post-Closing Responsibilities:

- **Property Transfer and Possession**: Complete property transfer and possession procedures according to the terms of the purchase agreement and closing documents. Coordinate with the seller, property management, and other stakeholders to ensure seamless transition and occupancy.

- **Loan Repayment and Servicing**: Fulfill loan repayment obligations according to the terms of the loan agreement. Set up loan servicing arrangements, establish automatic payments, and maintain regular communication with the lender to manage loan servicing effectively.

In summary, securing financing and closing deals require careful planning, preparation, and execution to successfully complete real estate transactions. By understanding financing options, navigating the loan approval process, coordinating closing logistics, and fulfilling post-closing responsibilities, investors can finalize property acquisitions, mitigate risks, and achieve their investment objectives in real estate markets.

5.4 Legal Considerations in Real Estate Transactions

Navigating legal considerations is essential in real estate transactions to ensure compliance with applicable laws, mitigate legal risks, and protect the interests of all parties involved. In this section, we explore key legal considerations that investors should address when engaging in real estate transactions.

1. Contractual Agreements:

- **Purchase Agreement**: Execute a legally binding purchase agreement that outlines the terms, conditions, and obligations of the real estate transaction. Include essential elements such as purchase price, closing date, financing contingencies, and property disclosures to clarify rights and responsibilities of both buyer and seller.

- **Contingencies**: Include contingencies in the purchase agreement to protect the buyer's interests and provide opportunities to withdraw from the transaction if certain conditions are not met. Common contingencies include financing contingencies, inspection contingencies, and appraisal contingencies.

2. Title and Ownership:

- **Title Examination**: Conduct a thorough title examination to verify ownership rights, identify any encumbrances or defects, and ensure clear and marketable title transfer. Obtain title insurance to protect against title defects, liens, or claims that may arise after closing.

- **Ownership Structures**: Determine the most suitable ownership structure for the property, such as sole ownership, joint tenancy, tenancy in common, or corporate ownership. Consult legal and tax professionals to evaluate the implications of each ownership structure on liability, taxation, and estate planning.

3. Disclosure Requirements:

- **Property Disclosures**: Comply with disclosure requirements mandated by state and federal laws to provide accurate and comprehensive disclosures regarding the property's condition, defects, hazards, and environmental risks. Failure to disclose material facts may result in legal liability and financial consequences for the seller.

- **Seller's Disclosures**: Provide sellers with statutory disclosure forms and questionnaires to collect relevant information about the property's history, maintenance, repairs, and known issues. Sellers must disclose material defects or conditions that may affect the property's value or desirability to potential buyers.

4. Financing and Mortgages:

- **Loan Documentation**: Review loan documents, including promissory notes, deeds of trust, and mortgage agreements, carefully to understand loan terms, repayment obligations, and consequences of default. Seek legal advice to clarify any ambiguities or legal implications of loan agreements.

- **Lender Requirements**: Comply with lender requirements and conditions, such as property appraisals, inspections, and insurance coverage, to satisfy loan underwriting criteria and secure mortgage financing. Fulfilling lender requirements is essential to facilitate loan approval and funding.

5. Closing Procedures:

- **Closing Documents**: Review and sign closing documents, including the settlement statement, deed, and transfer documents, in the presence of a notary public or closing agent. Ensure accuracy of information, verify compliance with contractual terms, and address any concerns before completing the closing process.

- **Funding and Disbursement**: Arrange for funding and disbursement of funds through escrow or closing agents to ensure timely and secure transfer of funds and property ownership. Confirm receipt of closing proceeds, payoffs, and prorated expenses according to the terms of the purchase agreement.

6. Legal Representation:

- **Legal Counsel**: Seek legal representation from qualified real estate attorneys to advise on legal matters, review contracts, and navigate complex legal issues arising in real estate transactions. Legal counsel provides expertise, protection, and advocacy to safeguard your interests and ensure compliance with applicable laws.

In summary, legal considerations are integral in real estate transactions to protect the rights, interests, and obligations of all parties involved. By addressing contractual agreements, title and ownership issues, disclosure requirements, financing arrangements, closing procedures, and securing legal representation, investors can navigate legal complexities effectively and mitigate legal risks in real estate transactions.

CHAPTER 6:

Property Management

Property management is essential for maintaining and maximizing the value of real estate investments. It involves tasks like tenant relations, maintenance, and financial oversight to ensure properties are well-maintained and profitable. Effective property management is key to achieving long-term success in real estate.

6.1 Effective Property Management Practices

Effective property management practices are essential for ensuring the long-term success and profitability of real estate investments. In this section, we explore key strategies and best practices that property managers can implement to optimize property performance, tenant satisfaction, and financial returns.

1. Comprehensive Tenant Screening:

- Conduct thorough background checks, credit evaluations, and rental history verifications to assess prospective tenants' suitability and reliability.
- Verify employment, income stability, and references to minimize the risk of rent defaults, lease violations, and tenant turnover.

2. Clear and Enforceable Lease Agreements:

- Draft clear and comprehensive lease agreements that outline tenant responsibilities, rental terms, and property rules.
- Enforce lease terms consistently and fairly, addressing lease violations promptly and in accordance with legal requirements.

3. Proactive Maintenance and Repairs:

- Implement regular property inspections to identify maintenance issues, safety hazards, and repair needs.

- Address maintenance and repair requests promptly, maintaining the property's condition, functionality, and value.

4. Effective Rent Collection and Financial Management:

- Establish streamlined rent collection processes, offering multiple payment options and enforcing rent due dates.
- Maintain accurate financial records, track income and expenses, and prepare timely financial reports to monitor property performance and profitability.

5. Responsive Tenant Communication:

- Foster open and transparent communication with tenants, addressing inquiries, concerns, and requests promptly.
- Provide multiple channels for communication, such as phone, email, and online portals, to accommodate tenant preferences and facilitate efficient resolution of issues.

6. Proactive Tenant Retention Strategies:

- Implement tenant retention programs, offering incentives, rewards, and lease renewal incentives to encourage lease extensions.
- Prioritize tenant satisfaction, addressing feedback, and proactively addressing concerns to cultivate long-term tenant relationships.

7. Legal Compliance and Risk Management:

- Stay informed about landlord-tenant laws, fair housing regulations, and local ordinances to ensure legal compliance.
- Mitigate legal risks by maintaining proper insurance coverage, conducting regular property inspections, and addressing safety and code compliance issues promptly.

8. Regular Property Inspections and Preventive Maintenance:

- Conduct routine property inspections to identify potential maintenance issues, safety hazards, and property improvements.
- Implement preventive maintenance schedules, addressing minor repairs and upkeep tasks to prevent costly damage and deterioration.

By implementing these effective property management practices, property managers can enhance property value, tenant satisfaction, and investment returns while minimizing risks and maximizing profitability in the competitive real estate market.

6.2 Tenant Screening and Relations

Tenant screening and relations are crucial aspects of effective property management, influencing tenant satisfaction, property performance, and overall investment success. In this section, we explore key strategies and best practices for tenant screening and fostering positive tenant relationships.

1. Comprehensive Tenant Screening:

- Conduct thorough background checks, including credit history, rental history, and criminal background, to assess prospective tenants' suitability and reliability.
- Verify employment, income stability, and references to ensure tenants have the financial means and character to fulfill lease obligations.

2. Transparent and Fair Application Process:

- Establish clear and transparent rental application procedures, outlining criteria, requirements, and fees for prospective tenants.
- Apply screening criteria consistently and fairly to all applicants, avoiding discrimination based on protected characteristics.

3. Effective Communication and Expectation Setting:

- Communicate rental policies, lease terms, and property rules clearly to prospective tenants during the application process.
- Set realistic expectations regarding tenant responsibilities, property maintenance, and community guidelines to prevent misunderstandings and disputes.

4. Proactive Tenant Relations:
- Foster positive tenant relations by being responsive, approachable, and proactive in addressing tenant inquiries, concerns, and requests.
- Establish multiple communication channels, such as phone, email, and online portals, to accommodate tenant preferences and facilitate efficient communication.

5. Tenant Retention Strategies:
- Implement tenant retention strategies to encourage lease renewals and minimize turnover, such as offering lease incentives, rewards programs, or renewal bonuses.

- Prioritize tenant satisfaction by addressing maintenance issues promptly, maintaining property amenities, and cultivating a sense of community.

6. Conflict Resolution and Dispute Management:
- Establish procedures for resolving tenant disputes and addressing conflicts, such as noise complaints, lease violations, or property damage.
- Mediate conflicts impartially, listening to both parties' perspectives and seeking amicable solutions to preserve tenant relationships and minimize disruptions.

7. Lease Renewal and Exit Processes:
- Initiate lease renewal discussions well in advance of lease expiration, offering renewal options and negotiating terms to retain valuable tenants.
- Facilitate smooth lease terminations and move-out processes, conducting final inspections, addressing security

deposit refunds, and preparing the unit for new occupancy.

By prioritizing effective tenant screening, transparent communication, proactive tenant relations, and conflict resolution, property managers can cultivate positive tenant experiences, minimize turnover, and enhance property performance and profitability in the competitive rental market.

6.3 Maintenance and Repairs

Maintenance and repairs are critical aspects of property management, ensuring that rental properties remain safe, functional, and attractive for tenants. In this section, we delve into key strategies and best practices for managing maintenance and repairs effectively.

1. Regular Maintenance Inspections:
- Conduct routine inspections of rental properties to identify any maintenance issues or repair needs.
- Schedule inspections on a regular basis, such as quarterly or

biannually, to catch problems early and prevent them from escalating.

2. Proactive Maintenance Planning:
- Develop a proactive maintenance plan that outlines regular upkeep tasks and preventive measures.
- Schedule routine maintenance for essential systems like HVAC, plumbing, and electrical to prolong their lifespan and minimize breakdowns.

3. Prompt Response to Repair Requests:
- Establish a system for tenants to report maintenance issues and respond to repair requests promptly.
- Prioritize urgent repairs, such as those affecting safety or habitability, to ensure tenant satisfaction and compliance with regulations.

4. Qualified Vendor Management:
- Build relationships with reliable contractors and service providers to

handle maintenance and repair tasks.
- Vet vendors carefully, ensuring they are licensed, insured, and capable of delivering quality workmanship.

5. Budgeting for Maintenance Expenses:
- Allocate funds for maintenance and repairs in the property budget to cover both routine upkeep and unexpected expenses.
- Monitor maintenance spending regularly and adjust the budget as needed to ensure adequate funds are available.

6. Compliance with Regulations:
- Stay informed about building codes, safety regulations, and landlord-tenant laws that govern maintenance and repair activities.
- Ensure all maintenance work complies with legal requirements and obtain necessary permits when required.

7. Communication with Tenants:

- Keep tenants informed about upcoming maintenance work, repair schedules, and any disruptions to normal operations.
- Provide clear instructions for submitting repair requests and communicate expectations for tenant cooperation during maintenance visits.

By prioritizing proactive maintenance, prompt repairs, and effective communication with tenants, property managers can ensure that rental properties remain well-maintained and attractive to tenants. Effective maintenance and repair management are essential for preserving property value, minimizing vacancies, and maximizing long-term investment returns.

6.4 Maximizing Cash Flow and ROI

Maximizing cash flow and return on investment (ROI) is the ultimate goal of real estate investment. In this section, we explore strategies and tactics to optimize cash flow and ROI in rental property management.

1. Rental Rate Optimization:
- Conduct market research to determine competitive rental rates for your property's location, size, and amenities.
- Adjust rental rates periodically to reflect market changes and maximize rental income without compromising tenant demand.

2. Expense Management:
- Monitor and control operating expenses, including property taxes, insurance, utilities, maintenance, and management fees.
- Implement cost-saving measures, such as energy-efficient upgrades and vendor negotiations, to minimize expenses and increase net operating income.

3. Tenant Retention:

- Prioritize tenant satisfaction and retention to minimize turnover and vacancy losses.
- Offer lease incentives, rewards programs, and responsive maintenance services to encourage long-term leases and reduce turnover costs.

4. Value-Add Strategies:
- Identify value-add opportunities to increase property value and rental income, such as renovations, upgrades, or additional amenities.
- Assess the cost-benefit of value-add projects and prioritize investments that yield the highest return on investment.

5. Financing Optimization:
- Evaluate financing options to minimize interest costs and maximize cash-on-cash returns.
- Consider refinancing existing mortgages, negotiating lower interest rates, or leveraging alternative

financing sources to optimize
financing terms.

6. Tax Planning:

- Utilize tax strategies and incentives
  to minimize tax liabilities and
  maximize after-tax cash flow.
- Take advantage of tax deductions,
  depreciation benefits, and 1031
  exchanges to optimize property tax
  efficiency and enhance overall ROI.

7. Proactive Asset Management:

- Monitor property performance
  regularly, analyzing financial metrics,
  occupancy rates, and market trends.
- Implement proactive asset
  management strategies to address
  issues, capitalize on opportunities,
  and maximize property value and
  ROI over time.

8. Portfolio Diversification:

- Diversify investment portfolios with a
  mix of property types, locations, and
  investment strategies to spread risk
  and enhance overall ROI.

- Allocate resources strategically across different asset classes to optimize cash flow, mitigate risk, and achieve long-term investment objectives.

By implementing these strategies and continually assessing property performance, investors can optimize cash flow, maximize ROI, and build wealth through real estate investment. Effective cash flow management is essential for sustaining profitability, supporting growth, and achieving financial success in real estate ownership.

CHAPTER 7:

Risk Management and Diversification

In real estate investment, risk management and diversification are essential strategies for protecting assets and optimizing returns. By spreading investments across diverse properties, locations, and asset classes, investors can mitigate risk and minimize the impact of market fluctuations. Additionally, implementing risk management practices, such as thorough due diligence, insurance coverage, and contingency planning, helps safeguard against unforeseen events and potential losses. Overall, combining risk management with diversification strategies enhances portfolio resilience and strengthens long-term investment performance in the dynamic real estate market.

7.1 Identifying and Mitigating Risks

Identifying and mitigating risks is crucial for successful real estate investment. In this section, we explore strategies to identify potential risks and implement measures to mitigate them effectively.

1. Market Risk Assessment:
- Conduct thorough market research to assess economic conditions, supply and demand dynamics, and market trends.
- Identify factors that may impact property values, rental demand, and investment returns, such as job growth, population trends, and development activity.

2. Property-Specific Risks:
- Perform comprehensive due diligence on potential investment properties, evaluating factors such as location, condition, zoning regulations, and environmental hazards.
- Identify property-specific risks, such as structural issues, legal

encumbrances, or potential liabilities, and develop mitigation strategies to address them.

3. Financial Risk Management:
- Evaluate financing options carefully, considering factors such as interest rates, loan terms, and leverage ratios.
- Implement financial risk management strategies, such as maintaining adequate cash reserves, diversifying financing sources, and avoiding over-leveraging.

4. Legal and Regulatory Compliance:
- Stay informed about local, state, and federal laws governing real estate transactions, landlord-tenant relationships, and property management.
- Ensure compliance with regulations, obtain necessary permits and licenses, and address legal issues promptly to mitigate legal risks.

5. Insurance Coverage:

- Obtain comprehensive insurance coverage for investment properties, including property insurance, liability insurance, and landlord insurance.
- Review insurance policies regularly, ensuring adequate coverage limits and understanding exclusions to mitigate financial risks associated with property damage or liability claims.

6. Contingency Planning:
- Develop contingency plans to address potential risks and unforeseen events, such as tenant vacancies, market downturns, or natural disasters.
- Maintain liquidity, establish emergency funds, and consider alternative exit strategies to navigate unexpected challenges and mitigate financial losses.

7. Professional Advice and Expertise:
- Seek guidance from real estate professionals, legal advisors, and financial experts to assess risks,

evaluate investment opportunities, and develop risk management strategies.
- Leverage their expertise and insights to make informed decisions, mitigate risks effectively, and optimize investment outcomes.

By identifying potential risks early, implementing proactive risk management strategies, and seeking professional guidance when needed, investors can minimize exposure to risk and enhance the resilience and profitability of their real estate investment portfolios.

7.2 Insurance Options for Real Estate Investors

Insurance is a crucial component of risk management for real estate investors, providing protection against various potential losses and liabilities. In this section, we explore different insurance options available to real estate investors to safeguard their investments effectively.

1. Property Insurance:

- Property insurance, also known as hazard insurance, covers physical damage to the investment property caused by perils such as fire, theft, vandalism, and natural disasters.
- Property insurance policies may vary in coverage levels and exclusions, so investors should carefully review policy terms and obtain adequate coverage based on property value and risk exposure.

2. Liability Insurance:

- Liability insurance protects real estate investors from legal liabilities arising from property-related accidents, injuries, or damages incurred by tenants, visitors, or third parties.
- Liability insurance typically covers costs associated with legal defense, settlements, and judgments, providing financial protection and peace of mind for investors.

3. Landlord Insurance:

- Landlord insurance is specifically designed for rental property owners, providing coverage for rental income loss, property damage, liability claims, and other risks associated with rental properties.
- Landlord insurance policies may include additional features such as coverage for tenant-caused damage, rental vacancy protection, and loss of rental income due to tenant defaults.

4. Umbrella Insurance:

- Umbrella insurance provides additional liability coverage beyond the limits of primary property and liability insurance policies.
- Umbrella policies offer higher coverage limits and broader protection against liability claims, making them valuable for real estate investors with substantial assets or exposure to higher risks.

5. Business Interruption Insurance:

- Business interruption insurance compensates real estate investors for lost rental income and operating expenses in the event of property damage or other covered perils that disrupt rental operations.
- Business interruption insurance helps mitigate financial losses during property repairs, tenant vacancies, or other interruptions to rental income streams.

6. Flood Insurance:
- Flood insurance provides coverage for property damage caused by floods, which are typically excluded from standard property insurance policies.
- Real estate investors in flood-prone areas or properties located in designated flood zones may be required to purchase flood insurance to protect their investments and comply with lender requirements.

7. Workers' Compensation Insurance:

- Workers' compensation insurance covers medical expenses, lost wages, and disability benefits for employees injured or disabled while performing work-related duties on the investment property.
- Real estate investors with employees, such as property managers or maintenance staff, may be required by law to carry workers' compensation insurance to protect both employees and the business.

By understanding the various insurance options available and tailoring coverage to their specific investment needs and risk exposures, real estate investors can effectively mitigate risks, protect their assets, and safeguard their financial interests in the dynamic real estate market.

7.3 Diversifying your Portfolio

Diversifying your real estate investment portfolio is a fundamental strategy for managing risk, maximizing returns, and achieving long-term financial success. In this section, we explore the importance of diversification and strategies to diversify your real estate investment portfolio effectively.

1. Asset Class Diversification:

- Invest in a variety of real estate asset classes, including residential, commercial, industrial, and mixed-use properties, to spread risk across different sectors and market segments.
- Each asset class offers unique risk-return profiles and may perform differently under various market conditions, providing opportunities for diversification and portfolio stability.

2. Geographic Diversification:

- Spread investments across different geographic locations, including diverse markets, regions, and neighborhoods, to mitigate the impact of local market fluctuations and economic downturns.

- Geographic diversification helps reduce concentration risk and exposure to specific geographic risks, such as natural disasters, regulatory changes, or economic downturns in a single market.

3. Property Type Diversification:
- Diversify your portfolio by investing in properties with different property types, such as single-family homes, multifamily apartment buildings, retail centers, office buildings, or industrial warehouses.
- Each property type has unique income streams, tenant demographics, and risk factors, allowing investors to balance their portfolio and capitalize on diverse investment opportunities.

4. Investment Strategy Diversification:
- Employ a mix of investment strategies, such as buy-and-hold, fix-and-flip, value-add, or development projects, to diversify

your investment approach and adapt to changing market conditions.
- Each investment strategy has its own risk-return characteristics and may perform differently in various market cycles, providing flexibility and resilience to your portfolio.

5. Risk Diversification:
- Identify and assess different types of risks, including market risk, liquidity risk, credit risk, and operational risk, and develop strategies to diversify and manage these risks effectively.
- By spreading investments across diverse assets, markets, and strategies, investors can reduce overall portfolio risk and enhance risk-adjusted returns over time.

6. Portfolio Rebalancing:
- Regularly review and rebalance your real estate investment portfolio to maintain diversification targets, adjust asset allocations, and reallocate resources based on

changing market conditions and investment objectives.

- Rebalancing helps optimize portfolio performance, mitigate risk, and align investments with long-term financial goals.

7. Professional Guidance:

- Seek advice from real estate professionals, financial advisors, and investment experts to develop a diversified investment strategy tailored to your risk tolerance, financial goals, and investment horizon.
- Leverage their expertise and insights to identify investment opportunities, assess risks, and build a resilient real estate investment portfolio.

By diversifying your real estate investment portfolio across different asset classes, geographic locations, property types, and investment strategies, you can reduce overall portfolio risk, enhance returns, and achieve greater stability and resilience in the face of market uncertainties.

Diversification is a cornerstone of sound investment management and is essential for long-term investment success in real estate.

7.4 Strategies for Market Volatility

Market volatility is an inherent aspect of real estate investment, influenced by various factors such as economic conditions, geopolitical events, and changes in investor sentiment. In this section, we explore strategies to navigate market volatility effectively and mitigate its impact on real estate investment portfolios.

1. Long-Term Investment Horizon:
- Adopt a long-term investment perspective and focus on fundamental factors such as property location, quality, and cash flow potential.
- Avoid making impulsive investment decisions based on short-term market fluctuations and instead

remain committed to your investment strategy and objectives.

2. Diversification:

- Diversify your real estate investment portfolio across different asset classes, geographic locations, and property types to spread risk and reduce exposure to specific market fluctuations.
- Diversification helps cushion the impact of market volatility and provides stability and resilience to your investment portfolio over time.

3. Cash Reserves:

- Maintain adequate cash reserves to weather periods of market uncertainty or economic downturns.
- Having sufficient liquidity allows you to capitalize on investment opportunities during market downturns, fund property improvements, or cover unexpected expenses without jeopardizing your portfolio.

4. Conservative Financing:

- Adopt conservative financing strategies, such as lower loan-to-value ratios and fixed-rate mortgages, to reduce financial leverage and minimize exposure to interest rate fluctuations.
- Avoid over-leveraging your investments, as excessive debt increases risk and may amplify losses during market downturns.

5. Value Investing:

- Focus on value investing principles, seeking properties that are undervalued or have the potential for future appreciation.
- Look for opportunities to acquire distressed assets, negotiate favorable purchase terms, and add value through renovations or operational improvements.

6. Active Portfolio Management:

- Monitor market conditions regularly and adjust your investment strategy

as needed to capitalize on opportunities and mitigate risks.
- Consider reallocating resources, rebalancing your portfolio, or diversifying into alternative asset classes to adapt to changing market dynamics.

7. Professional Advice:
- Seek guidance from real estate professionals, financial advisors, and investment experts to navigate market volatility effectively.
- Consult with professionals to assess market conditions, evaluate investment opportunities, and develop strategies to manage risk and optimize returns.

8. Maintain a Long-Term Perspective:
- Recognize that market volatility is a normal part of investing and focus on your long-term financial goals and objectives.
- Stay disciplined and patient during periods of market turbulence, avoiding knee-jerk reactions or

emotional decision-making that may undermine your investment strategy.

By implementing these strategies and maintaining a disciplined approach to real estate investment, investors can navigate market volatility effectively, preserve capital, and achieve long-term financial success in the dynamic real estate market.

CHAPTER 8:

Exit Strategies and Portfolio Optimization

Exit strategies are essential components of real estate investment planning, allowing investors to capitalize on opportunities, mitigate risks, and optimize portfolio performance. Whether aiming to realize profits, rebalance investments, or adapt to changing market conditions, having a well-defined exit strategy is crucial for achieving investment objectives. Portfolio optimization involves continuously evaluating and adjusting investment holdings to maximize returns while minimizing risk. By strategically reallocating resources, rebalancing asset allocations, and divesting underperforming properties, investors can enhance portfolio resilience and adapt to evolving market dynamics. Exit strategies and portfolio optimization are integral parts of effective investment management, ensuring that investors can capitalize on opportunities, mitigate risks, and achieve long-term financial success in the competitive real estate market.

8.1 Selling vs. Holding Properties

Deciding whether to sell or hold investment properties is a critical consideration for real estate investors, influenced by various factors such as market conditions, investment objectives, and financial goals. In this section, we explore the key considerations and factors to weigh when evaluating the decision to sell or hold properties.

1. Market Conditions:
- Assess current market conditions, including property values, demand trends, and economic indicators, to determine the optimal timing for selling or holding properties.
- Consider factors such as supply and demand dynamics, interest rates, and local market trends to gauge market sentiment and identify opportunities.

2. Investment Objectives:

- Clarify your investment objectives and goals, whether they involve short-term profit maximization, long-term wealth accumulation, or income generation.
- Align your decision to sell or hold properties with your investment strategy and objectives, balancing risk and return considerations.

3. Cash Flow and Income:

- Evaluate the cash flow and income potential of investment properties, considering rental income, operating expenses, and potential vacancy risks.
- Determine whether holding properties generates sufficient cash flow to meet your financial needs and objectives or if selling properties would unlock additional capital for other investment opportunities.

4. Capital Appreciation:

- Assess the potential for capital appreciation of investment properties over time, based on market appreciation trends, property improvements, and demand drivers.
- Compare the expected returns from holding properties with the potential gains from selling properties at current market values to optimize portfolio performance.

5. Tax Implications:
- Consider the tax implications of selling investment properties, including capital gains taxes, depreciation recapture, and potential tax benefits.
- Consult with tax advisors or financial professionals to assess the tax consequences of selling properties and explore strategies to minimize tax liabilities.

6. Portfolio Diversification:
- Evaluate the impact of selling or holding properties on portfolio diversification, considering the overall

asset allocation, risk exposure, and investment mix.
- Determine whether selling properties would help rebalance the portfolio, reduce concentration risk, or reallocate resources to alternative investments.

7. Opportunity Cost:
- Assess the opportunity cost of holding properties versus selling properties and deploying capital elsewhere, considering factors such as alternative investment opportunities, liquidity needs, and risk-adjusted returns.
- Compare the expected returns from holding properties with the potential gains from alternative investments to make informed decisions.

8. Long-Term Investment Strategy:
- Evaluate the alignment of selling or holding properties with your long-term investment strategy and objectives, considering factors such

as market cycles, economic outlook, and future growth prospects.

- Determine whether selling properties aligns with your investment horizon, risk tolerance, and overall financial plan or if holding properties would better support your long-term wealth accumulation goals.

By carefully weighing these considerations and evaluating the unique circumstances of each investment property, investors can make informed decisions regarding whether to sell or hold properties to optimize portfolio performance and achieve their financial objectives.

8.2 Timing the Market for Maximum Profit

Timing the real estate market is a key factor in maximizing profit and optimizing investment returns. In this section, we delve into strategies and considerations for effectively timing the market to achieve maximum profit when buying and selling investment properties.

1. Market Research and Analysis:

- Conduct comprehensive market research to understand current market conditions, trends, and forecasts.
- Analyze factors such as supply and demand dynamics, economic indicators, interest rates, and local market trends to gauge market sentiment and identify optimal timing opportunities.

2. Market Cycles and Trends:

- Study market cycles and trends to identify patterns and anticipate market movements.
- Recognize the stages of the real estate market cycle, including expansion, peak, contraction, and recovery, and adjust investment strategies accordingly.

3. Buyer and Seller Behavior:

- Pay attention to buyer and seller behavior to gauge market sentiment and investor confidence.
- Monitor factors such as inventory levels, days on market, and bidding activity to assess market dynamics and identify buying or selling opportunities.

4. Seasonal Variations:
- Consider seasonal variations in real estate activity and market trends.
- Recognize peak seasons for buying and selling properties and leverage seasonal fluctuations to maximize profit potential.

5. Economic Indicators:
- Monitor economic indicators such as GDP growth, employment rates, inflation, and consumer confidence to gauge overall economic health and its impact on real estate markets.
- Anticipate changes in interest rates, monetary policy, and fiscal stimulus measures that may affect market conditions and investment decisions.

6. Local Market Analysis:

- Conduct in-depth analysis of local market conditions, including neighborhood trends, property values, and demographic factors.
- Identify emerging neighborhoods, development opportunities, and areas of growth potential to capitalize on market trends and maximize profit.

7. Flexibility and Adaptability:

- Remain flexible and adaptable in response to changing market conditions and unforeseen events.
- Adjust investment strategies, pricing strategies, and timelines based on evolving market dynamics and investment objectives.

8. Risk Management:

- Implement risk management strategies to protect against potential losses and downside risk.
- Diversify investment holdings, maintain liquidity, and consider

hedging strategies or contingency plans to mitigate risks associated with market timing.

By carefully timing the real estate market and leveraging market trends, cycles, and indicators, investors can maximize profit potential, optimize investment returns, and achieve long-term financial success in real estate investment.

8.3 1031 Exchange and Tax Deferral Strategies

Utilizing tax-deferral strategies such as the 1031 exchange is a powerful tool for real estate investors to optimize their investment returns and manage tax liabilities. In this section, we explore the benefits of 1031 exchanges and other tax deferral strategies to maximize wealth accumulation and portfolio growth.

1. 1031 Exchange Basics:
- Understand the fundamentals of a 1031 exchange, which allows

investors to defer capital gains taxes on the sale of investment properties by reinvesting the proceeds into like-kind properties.

- Familiarize yourself with IRS regulations and requirements for 1031 exchanges, including deadlines for identifying replacement properties and completing the exchange process.

2. Tax Deferral Benefits:

- Appreciate the tax-deferral benefits of a 1031 exchange, which enable investors to defer capital gains taxes and depreciation recapture taxes, allowing for greater reinvestment of capital and portfolio growth.
- Recognize how tax deferral strategies can enhance cash flow, increase purchasing power, and accelerate wealth accumulation over time.

3. Replacement Property Identification:

- Strategically identify replacement properties that align with your investment objectives and meet the requirements for a 1031 exchange.

- Consider factors such as property type, location, cash flow potential, and appreciation prospects when selecting replacement properties to maximize investment returns.

4. Portfolio Diversification:

- Utilize 1031 exchanges to diversify your real estate investment portfolio by exchanging properties in one market or asset class for properties in different markets or asset classes.
- Leverage 1031 exchanges to rebalance your portfolio, consolidate holdings, or acquire properties with greater income potential or growth prospects.

5. Reverse and Improvement Exchanges:

- Explore alternative 1031 exchange strategies such as reverse exchanges and improvement exchanges to accommodate specific

investment goals or property acquisition challenges.
- Understand the requirements and complexities of reverse and improvement exchanges, including financing considerations, timing constraints, and compliance with IRS regulations.

6. Tax Planning and Consultation:
- Consult with tax advisors, legal experts, and qualified intermediaries to develop tax-efficient strategies and maximize the benefits of 1031 exchanges.
- Evaluate the tax implications of various investment scenarios, assess the long-term tax consequences of exchange transactions, and implement strategies to optimize tax savings.

7. Exit Strategies and Long-Term Planning:
- Incorporate 1031 exchanges into your exit strategy and long-term investment planning to manage tax

liabilities and optimize portfolio performance.
- Consider the timing of 1031 exchanges, potential future tax implications, and overall investment objectives when structuring exchange transactions.

8. Compliance and Documentation:
- Ensure compliance with IRS regulations and documentation requirements throughout the 1031 exchange process, including proper identification of replacement properties, completion of exchange documents, and timely reporting of transactions.
- Maintain accurate records and documentation to support exchange transactions and facilitate tax reporting and audit compliance.

By leveraging 1031 exchanges and other tax deferral strategies effectively, real estate investors can defer capital gains taxes, preserve investment capital, and accelerate portfolio growth while maximizing long-term wealth accumulation and investment returns.

8.4 Reinvesting Profits for Portfolio Growth

Reinvesting profits is a fundamental strategy for portfolio growth and wealth accumulation in real estate investment. In this section, we explore the benefits and strategies for reinvesting profits to maximize portfolio growth and enhance long-term investment returns.

1. Compounding Returns:
- Harness the power of compounding returns by reinvesting profits from real estate investments into additional properties or asset classes.
- Reinvesting profits allows investors to accelerate portfolio growth and compound investment returns over time, leading to exponential wealth accumulation.

2. Property Acquisition:

- Allocate profits towards acquiring additional investment properties that offer strong cash flow potential, appreciation prospects, or value-add opportunities.
- Diversify your real estate investment portfolio by acquiring properties in different markets, asset classes, or geographic locations to spread risk and maximize growth potential.

3. Portfolio Expansion:

- Expand your real estate investment portfolio by reinvesting profits into larger-scale projects, development opportunities, or income-producing assets.
- Explore opportunities to scale up your investment activities and leverage economies of scale to enhance portfolio performance and profitability.

4. Capital Improvements:

- Reinvest profits into property improvements, renovations, or

upgrades to enhance asset value, attract higher-quality tenants, and increase rental income.
- Implement value-add strategies to maximize the return on investment from capital improvements and enhance the overall performance of investment properties.

5. Debt Reduction:
- Use profits to pay down existing debt or mortgages on investment properties to improve cash flow, reduce financing costs, and strengthen financial stability.
- Debt reduction strategies help lower leverage ratios, mitigate financial risk, and increase equity positions in investment properties over time.

6. Reserve Funds:
- Allocate a portion of profits towards establishing reserve funds for property maintenance, repairs, or unexpected expenses.
- Maintaining adequate reserve funds ensures liquidity and financial

stability, allowing investors to weather economic downturns or unforeseen challenges without compromising portfolio performance.

7. Tax-Deferred Investments:

- Explore tax-deferred investment vehicles such as retirement accounts, like self-directed IRAs or solo 401(k)s, to reinvest profits from real estate transactions without immediate tax consequences.
- Utilize tax-deferred investment strategies to optimize after-tax returns, preserve capital, and maximize wealth accumulation over the long term.

8. Strategic Planning and Analysis:

- Develop a strategic reinvestment plan based on thorough analysis of market conditions, investment opportunities, and financial objectives.
- Continuously evaluate investment alternatives, assess risk-return trade-offs, and adjust reinvestment

strategies to align with changing market dynamics and investment goals.

By reinvesting profits strategically and proactively, real estate investors can accelerate portfolio growth, optimize investment returns, and build long-term wealth and financial security. Reinvesting profits is a cornerstone of successful real estate investment and is essential for achieving and sustaining investment success in the dynamic real estate market.

CHAPTER 9:

Scaling Your Investments

Scaling your investments in real estate involves systematically increasing the size and profitability of your portfolio. This is achieved through strategic planning, disciplined execution, and continuous learning. By diversifying assets, optimizing finances, and seizing growth opportunities, investors can accelerate wealth accumulation and achieve their long-term financial goals.

9.1 Growing Your Real Estate Portfolio

Growing your real estate portfolio is a dynamic process that involves acquiring new properties, optimizing existing assets, and expanding investment opportunities. In this section, we explore strategies and tactics for effectively growing your real estate portfolio to increase wealth and achieve long-term financial success.

1. Strategic Acquisition:
- Identify strategic opportunities to acquire new properties that align with your investment objectives and portfolio growth strategy.
- Conduct thorough market research, financial analysis, and due diligence to evaluate potential investment opportunities and mitigate risks.

2. Value-Add Investments:
- Focus on value-add investments that offer opportunities for renovation, redevelopment, or operational improvements to enhance property value and rental income.
- Implement value-add strategies to maximize returns and optimize the performance of existing assets within your portfolio.

3. Portfolio Diversification:
- Diversify your real estate portfolio by investing in different asset classes,

geographic locations, and property types to spread risk and maximize growth potential.

- Balance your portfolio with a mix of income-producing properties, growth-oriented assets, and value-add opportunities to optimize risk-adjusted returns.

4. Financing Strategies:

- Explore financing options such as traditional mortgages, private loans, or creative financing solutions to fund property acquisitions and portfolio expansion.
- Optimize financing structures, negotiate favorable terms, and leverage financial leverage to maximize purchasing power and accelerate portfolio growth.

5. Market Expansion:

- Expand your real estate portfolio into new markets or geographic regions with strong growth potential, favorable supply-demand dynamics,

and attractive investment
fundamentals.
- Conduct market research, establish
local partnerships, and build
networks to facilitate market entry
and navigate regulatory
requirements.

6. Active Management:

- Implement proactive management
strategies to optimize property
performance, maximize rental
income, and enhance operational
efficiency within your portfolio.
- Stay engaged with tenants, address
maintenance issues promptly, and
leverage technology to streamline
property management processes and
improve tenant satisfaction.

7. Reinvestment of Profits:

- Reinvest profits from property sales,
refinancing, or cash flow into
acquiring new properties or funding
capital improvements to existing
assets.

- Continuously reinvesting profits allows for portfolio growth, compounding returns, and accelerating wealth accumulation over time.

8. Long-Term Vision:
- Maintain a long-term perspective and focus on sustainable growth and wealth creation when growing your real estate portfolio.
- Set clear investment goals, develop a strategic roadmap, and stay committed to your vision despite short-term challenges or market fluctuations.

By implementing these strategies and tactics, investors can effectively grow their real estate portfolio, increase wealth, and achieve their long-term financial objectives in the dynamic real estate market.

9.2 Leveraging Equity and Financing Options

Leveraging equity and exploring financing options are essential strategies for expanding your real estate portfolio and maximizing investment returns. In this section, we delve into the various ways investors can leverage equity and utilize financing to grow their real estate investments effectively.

1. Equity Leveraging:
- Utilize existing equity in your real estate assets to acquire new properties or fund capital improvements through equity leveraging strategies.
- Extract equity from properties through cash-out refinancing, home equity lines of credit (HELOCs), or equity partnerships to access capital for new investments.

2. Mortgage Financing:
- Secure mortgage financing from traditional lenders, such as banks or

credit unions, to fund property
acquisitions or refinancing existing
mortgages.
- Explore different mortgage options,
including fixed-rate mortgages,
adjustable-rate mortgages (ARMs),
or government-backed loans, to find
the most suitable financing solution
for your investment goals.

3. Private Lending:
- Consider private lending options,
such as hard money loans or private
investors, to access capital quickly
for short-term investment
opportunities or distressed property
acquisitions.
- Private lending offers flexibility,
speed, and accessibility for investors
seeking alternative financing options
outside of traditional banking
channels.

4. Seller Financing:
- Negotiate seller financing
arrangements with property sellers to
acquire properties with minimal

upfront capital and flexible payment terms.

- Seller financing allows investors to bypass traditional lending institutions, negotiate favorable terms directly with sellers, and structure creative financing solutions tailored to specific investment needs.

5. Equity Partnerships:

- Form equity partnerships with other investors or real estate syndicates to pool resources, share risks, and access larger investment opportunities.
- Equity partnerships allow investors to leverage collective capital, expertise, and networks to pursue larger-scale projects or diversify investment portfolios across multiple properties or asset classes.

6. Creative Financing Structures:

- Explore creative financing structures, such as lease options, seller carry-back financing, or wraparound mortgages, to facilitate property

acquisitions and overcome financing challenges.
- Creative financing structures offer flexibility, customization, and innovative solutions for investors navigating complex real estate transactions or unique investment scenarios.

7. Portfolio Optimization:
- Continuously optimize your real estate portfolio by refinancing existing mortgages, consolidating debt, or restructuring financing arrangements to improve cash flow, reduce financing costs, and maximize returns.
- Regularly review financing options, monitor interest rate trends, and adapt financing strategies to align with changing market conditions and investment objectives.

8. Risk Management:
- Implement risk management strategies to mitigate financing risks, including interest rate fluctuations,

payment defaults, or liquidity constraints.

- Maintain adequate reserves, diversify financing sources, and conduct stress tests to assess the impact of adverse scenarios on portfolio performance and financial stability.

By leveraging equity and exploring a range of financing options, investors can unlock new opportunities, accelerate portfolio growth, and optimize investment returns in the dynamic real estate market. Strategic use of leverage and financing is a cornerstone of successful real estate investment and is essential for achieving long-term financial success and wealth accumulation.

9.3 Expanding into New Markets

Expanding into new markets is a strategic approach for diversifying real estate investments, accessing growth opportunities, and maximizing portfolio performance. In this section, we explore the considerations and strategies for successfully expanding into new markets.

1. Market Research and Analysis:
- Conduct comprehensive market research to identify potential new markets with favorable investment fundamentals, including economic growth, population trends, job markets, and demographic shifts.
- Analyze market dynamics, supply-demand fundamentals, rental trends, and regulatory environments to assess the viability and attractiveness of new markets for real estate investment.

2. Risk Assessment:
- Evaluate the risks and challenges associated with expanding into new markets, including unfamiliarity with local regulations, economic volatility, political instability, and competitive landscapes.
- Develop risk mitigation strategies, establish contingency plans, and allocate resources prudently to

manage risks effectively when entering new markets.

3. Local Partnerships and Networks:
- Establish partnerships with local real estate professionals, property managers, brokers, and industry experts to gain insights, access market intelligence, and navigate local nuances.
- Leverage local networks and relationships to identify investment opportunities, secure financing, and streamline operational processes when expanding into new markets.

4. Property Selection Criteria:
- Define clear investment criteria and property selection parameters tailored to the dynamics of each new market, considering factors such as property type, location, asset class, and investment strategy.
- Prioritize properties that align with your investment goals, risk tolerance, and financial objectives to optimize

portfolio performance and mitigate investment risks.

5. Due Diligence and Site Visits:

- Conduct thorough due diligence on potential investment properties in new markets, including property inspections, financial analysis, title searches, and environmental assessments.
- Visit target markets personally to assess local conditions, neighborhoods, and investment opportunities firsthand, gaining valuable insights and building confidence in investment decisions.

6. Market Entry Strategy:

- Develop a strategic market entry plan outlining goals, timelines, and action steps for expanding into new markets.
- Consider entry strategies such as direct property acquisitions, joint ventures, partnerships, or acquisitions of existing portfolios to

establish a presence and gain traction in new markets.

7. Adaptation and Flexibility:

- Remain adaptable and flexible in response to evolving market conditions, regulatory changes, and unforeseen challenges when expanding into new markets.
- Adjust strategies, refine approaches, and leverage lessons learned from previous experiences to optimize performance and achieve success in new market environments.

8. Long-Term Commitment:

- Approach expansion into new markets with a long-term perspective and commitment to building sustainable, scalable real estate investments.
- Allocate resources, invest in local relationships, and cultivate a deep understanding of new markets to foster growth, capitalize on opportunities, and achieve long-term financial objectives.

By following these strategies and considerations, investors can successfully expand into new markets, diversify their real estate portfolios, and capitalize on growth opportunities to achieve long-term financial success and wealth accumulation. Expanding into new markets requires careful planning, diligent execution, and a willingness to adapt to changing market dynamics, but the potential rewards can be significant for savvy investors.

9.4 Building a Team for Success

Building a competent and reliable team is crucial for achieving success and maximizing returns in real estate investment. In this section, we explore the importance of assembling a skilled team and the key roles necessary for driving success in real estate ventures.

1. Identify Core Team Members:
- Define the key roles required for your real estate investment ventures,

including property management, legal, financial, and construction expertise.
- Identify individuals with the necessary skills, experience, and qualifications to fulfill these roles effectively and contribute to the success of your investments.

2. Property Management:
- Hire or partner with experienced property managers who can oversee day-to-day operations, tenant relations, maintenance, and financial management of your investment properties.
- Ensure property managers are responsive, proactive, and capable of maximizing rental income, minimizing vacancies, and preserving property value.

3. Legal Counsel:
- Retain legal counsel specializing in real estate law to provide guidance on property acquisitions, contract

negotiations, lease agreements, and regulatory compliance.
- Ensure legal advisors are familiar with local laws and regulations governing real estate transactions to mitigate legal risks and protect your interests.

4. Financial Advisors:
- Engage financial advisors, accountants, or tax professionals with expertise in real estate investment to optimize financial strategies, tax planning, and asset protection.
- Work with financial experts to structure financing arrangements, manage cash flow, and maximize returns while minimizing tax liabilities and compliance risks.

5. Construction and Renovation Experts:
- Collaborate with construction professionals, architects, and contractors to execute property

renovations, improvements, or redevelopment projects effectively.
- Ensure construction partners have the necessary experience, resources, and track record to deliver quality workmanship on time and within budget.

6. Networking and Partnerships:
- Cultivate relationships with industry peers, mentors, and service providers to access valuable insights, resources, and support networks within the real estate community.
- Leverage networking opportunities to identify potential team members, collaborate on joint ventures, and share knowledge and best practices for mutual benefit.

7. Communication and Collaboration:
- Foster open communication, transparency, and collaboration among team members to facilitate effective decision-making, problem-solving, and project execution.

- Establish clear expectations, roles, and responsibilities for each team member, and maintain regular communication channels to ensure alignment and accountability.

8. Continuous Learning and Development:

- Invest in ongoing education, training, and professional development for yourself and your team members to stay abreast of industry trends, regulations, and best practices.
- Encourage a culture of continuous improvement, innovation, and adaptability to navigate evolving market dynamics and seize new opportunities for growth and success.

By building a competent and collaborative team, real estate investors can leverage diverse expertise, mitigate risks, and maximize returns on investment. A well-rounded team is essential for overcoming challenges, seizing opportunities, and achieving long-term success in the dynamic and competitive real estate market.

CHAPTER 10:

Advanced Investment Strategies

Advanced investment strategies in real estate involve sophisticated approaches to maximize returns, manage risks, and achieve financial goals. These strategies often entail leveraging complex financial instruments, employing innovative tactics, and implementing tailored solutions to capitalize on market inefficiencies and unlock value. Investors pursuing advanced strategies must possess a deep understanding of market dynamics, regulatory environments, and financial principles to navigate complexities successfully. While offering potential for higher returns, advanced investment strategies also entail greater risks and require careful planning, expertise, and diligent execution to mitigate downside and optimize performance.

10.1 Commercial Real Estate Investing

Commercial real estate investing involves acquiring, owning, and managing income-producing properties such as office buildings, retail centers, industrial warehouses, and multifamily complexes. In this section, we explore the fundamentals of commercial real estate investing and strategies for success in this dynamic sector.

1. Property Types:
- Understand the various types of commercial properties, including office, retail, industrial, hospitality, and multifamily, each with its unique characteristics, risks, and potential returns.
- Evaluate market demand, tenant profiles, and economic drivers specific to each property type to identify investment opportunities aligned with your investment objectives.

2. Market Analysis:

- Conduct thorough market analysis to assess supply and demand dynamics, vacancy rates, rental trends, and competitive landscapes within target markets.
- Evaluate economic indicators, demographic trends, and regulatory factors impacting commercial real estate markets to gauge investment viability and mitigate risks.

3. Financing Strategies:

- Explore financing options tailored to commercial real estate investments, such as commercial mortgages, bridge loans, mezzanine financing, or syndicated debt.
- Assess loan-to-value ratios, debt service coverage ratios, and interest rate terms to optimize financing structures and enhance returns while managing leverage risks.

4. Tenant Relations:

- Develop tenant relations strategies to attract and retain quality tenants,

negotiate favorable lease terms, and minimize vacancies within commercial properties.
- Implement proactive property management practices, responsive tenant services, and tenant improvement incentives to enhance tenant satisfaction and maximize rental income.

5. Lease Negotiation:
- Negotiate lease agreements with tenants to secure long-term, stable cash flow and mitigate risks associated with tenant turnover or lease defaults.
- Structure lease terms, rent escalations, renewal options, and tenant improvements to align with market conditions, property performance, and investment objectives.

6. Value-Add Opportunities:
- Identify value-add opportunities within commercial properties, such as renovation, repositioning, or

redevelopment projects, to enhance
asset value and maximize returns.
- Implement strategic improvements,
  capital investments, and operational
  enhancements to optimize property
  performance and attract
  higher-quality tenants.

7. Risk Management:
- Mitigate risks associated with
  commercial real estate investments
  by diversifying across property types,
  geographic locations, and tenant
  profiles.
- Maintain adequate reserves,
  insurance coverage, and contingency
  plans to address operational,
  financial, and market-related risks
  effectively.

8. Exit Strategies:
- Develop exit strategies tailored to
  commercial real estate investments,
  such as property disposition,
  refinancing, or portfolio repositioning,
  to optimize liquidity and maximize
  returns.

- Evaluate market conditions, investment performance, and capital market trends to determine optimal timing and execution of exit strategies aligned with investment objectives.

Commercial real estate investing offers opportunities for income generation, wealth accumulation, and portfolio diversification for savvy investors. By understanding market dynamics, implementing sound investment strategies, and managing risks effectively, investors can achieve success and build long-term wealth in the dynamic commercial real estate sector.

10.2 Real Estate Syndication and Partnerships

Real estate syndication and partnerships involve pooling resources, expertise, and capital from multiple investors to acquire, manage, and profit from investment properties. In this section, we explore the fundamentals of real estate syndication and partnerships and the benefits they offer to investors.

1. Syndication Structure:

- Understand the structure of real estate syndication, which typically involves a general partner (sponsor) who manages the investment and limited partners (investors) who contribute capital.
- Determine the roles, responsibilities, and profit-sharing arrangements among syndicate members to align interests and optimize returns.

2. Access to Deals:

- Gain access to larger-scale investment opportunities and high-quality properties that may be beyond the reach of individual investors through syndication and partnerships.
- Benefit from the sponsor's expertise, market knowledge, and deal sourcing capabilities to identify and underwrite attractive investment opportunities.

3. Diversification:

- Diversify investment portfolios across multiple properties, asset classes, and geographic locations through participation in real estate syndicates and partnerships.
- Spread risk and minimize exposure to individual property or market-specific risks by investing in a diversified portfolio managed by experienced sponsors.

4. Expertise and Management:

- Leverage the expertise, experience, and track record of sponsors and syndicate managers to navigate complex real estate transactions, mitigate risks, and optimize property performance.
- Delegate property management, leasing, and operational responsibilities to professional teams and partners to maximize efficiency and profitability.

5. Passive Income and Cash Flow:

- Generate passive income and cash flow distributions from real estate investments without the day-to-day management responsibilities typically associated with property ownership.
- Receive regular distributions of rental income, proceeds from property sales, and other investment returns based on the syndication agreement and investment structure.

6. Risk Mitigation:
- Mitigate investment risks through due diligence, underwriting standards, and risk-sharing mechanisms embedded in syndication agreements.
- Benefit from economies of scale, diversification benefits, and shared resources to minimize downside risk and enhance overall portfolio resilience.

7. Tax Benefits:
- Access tax advantages associated with real estate ownership, including depreciation deductions, mortgage

interest deductions, and capital gains tax deferral opportunities available to syndicate members.

- Structure investments to optimize tax efficiency and maximize after-tax returns for investors while complying with applicable tax regulations.

8. Exit Strategies:

- Plan exit strategies and liquidity events for real estate syndication investments, such as property sales, refinancing, or portfolio liquidation, to unlock value and distribute profits to investors.
- Evaluate market conditions, investment performance, and investor preferences to determine the most appropriate timing and approach for exiting syndicated investments.

Real estate syndication and partnerships offer investors opportunities to access high-quality real estate investments, diversify portfolios, and generate passive income while leveraging the expertise and resources of experienced sponsors. By participating in syndicated deals, investors can achieve their investment objectives and build wealth through collaborative and professionally managed real estate investments.

10.3 Real Estate Investment Trusts (REITs)

Real Estate Investment Trusts (REITs) provide investors with a unique opportunity to invest in income-generating real estate assets while enjoying the benefits of liquidity, diversification, and professional management. In this section, we delve into the features, benefits, and considerations of investing in REITs.

1. Structure and Operation:
- Understand the structure of REITs, which are publicly traded companies that own, operate, or finance income-producing real estate assets across various sectors, including

commercial, residential, and
industrial properties.
- REITs typically distribute a significant
portion of their taxable income to
shareholders in the form of
dividends, allowing investors to
benefit from regular income streams.

2. Diversification:

- Gain exposure to a diversified
portfolio of real estate assets and
properties across different
geographic regions, sectors, and
property types through investment in
REITs.
- Diversification reduces concentration
risk and enhances portfolio resilience
by spreading investment across a
broad spectrum of real estate assets.

3. Liquidity:

- Enjoy liquidity and tradability of REIT
shares on public stock exchanges,
providing investors with the flexibility
to buy and sell shares easily without
the constraints of traditional real
estate investments.

- Access to liquidity allows investors to adjust portfolio allocations, rebalance holdings, and capitalize on market opportunities swiftly and efficiently.

4. Passive Income:
- Generate passive income and cash flow through regular dividends distributed by REITs, which are derived from rental income, property sales, and financing activities.
- REIT dividends are typically higher than those of other equities and may offer attractive income yields for income-oriented investors.

5. Professional Management:
- Benefit from professional management and expertise of REIT management teams responsible for property acquisition, leasing, asset management, and financial operations.
- REIT managers employ rigorous due diligence, underwriting standards, and risk management practices to

optimize property performance and enhance shareholder value.

6. Tax Efficiency:

- Enjoy tax advantages associated with REIT investments, including pass-through taxation, which allows REITs to avoid corporate income tax by distributing a significant portion of taxable income to shareholders.
- Investors may also benefit from favorable tax treatment on dividends received from REITs, including potential qualified dividend tax rates for eligible investors.

7. Transparency and Regulation:

- Benefit from transparency, regulatory oversight, and reporting requirements imposed on REITs by securities regulators and stock exchanges to protect investor interests and ensure accountability.
- REITs are subject to stringent regulatory standards, including asset diversification, income distribution, and corporate governance

requirements, to maintain their status as tax-advantaged investment vehicles.

8. Growth Potential:

- Participate in the growth potential of real estate markets and sectors through investment in REITs, which have the ability to acquire, develop, and manage properties to capitalize on market opportunities and enhance shareholder value.
- REITs may pursue growth strategies such as property acquisitions, development projects, and portfolio expansion to generate long-term capital appreciation for investors.

Real Estate Investment Trusts (REITs) offer investors an efficient and accessible way to invest in real estate assets and participate in the income and growth potential of the real estate sector. By incorporating REITs into their investment portfolios, investors can achieve diversification, income generation, and long-term wealth accumulation in a tax-efficient and professionally managed manner.

10.4 International Real Estate Opportunities

International real estate investments offer investors the potential for diversification, capital appreciation, and exposure to dynamic global markets. In this section, we explore the opportunities, considerations, and strategies for investing in international real estate.

1. Market Selection:
- Evaluate potential international real estate markets based on factors such as economic stability, political environment, regulatory framework, currency stability, and property rights protection.
- Conduct thorough market research and due diligence to assess market fundamentals, growth prospects, and investment risks in target countries or regions.

2. Property Types:

- Consider investing in various types of international real estate assets, including residential properties, commercial buildings, office spaces, retail centers, hospitality properties, and industrial warehouses.
- Select property types that align with your investment goals, risk tolerance, and market dynamics in target international markets.

3. Currency Exchange Considerations:

- Assess currency exchange rates, foreign exchange risks, and currency hedging strategies when investing in international real estate to mitigate currency-related risks and preserve investment value.
- Monitor currency trends, geopolitical developments, and macroeconomic factors that may impact currency fluctuations and investment returns.

4. Legal and Regulatory Environment:

- Understand the legal and regulatory environment governing real estate ownership, investment structures, tax implications, and foreign investor rights in target international markets.
- Seek legal counsel and local expertise to navigate legal complexities, compliance requirements, and regulatory nuances when investing in foreign real estate.

5. Cultural and Market Differences:
- Recognize cultural differences, market practices, and business customs in international real estate markets to effectively negotiate deals, build relationships, and navigate local dynamics.
- Adapt investment strategies, communication styles, and operational approaches to align with cultural norms and market expectations in foreign jurisdictions.

6. Risk Management:

- Mitigate risks associated with international real estate investments through diversification, thorough due diligence, and risk mitigation strategies tailored to specific market conditions and investment objectives.
- Assess political risks, economic volatility, market liquidity, and geopolitical factors that may impact investment performance and implement risk management measures accordingly.

7. Local Partnerships and Networks:
- Establish local partnerships, alliances, and networks with real estate professionals, developers, brokers, and service providers in target international markets to gain insights, access opportunities, and navigate local challenges.
- Leverage local expertise, market knowledge, and relationships to identify investment opportunities, conduct due diligence, and execute transactions effectively.

8. Exit Strategies:

- Develop exit strategies and contingency plans for international real estate investments, including property sales, portfolio liquidation, or repatriation of capital, to optimize returns and manage liquidity.
- Evaluate market conditions, currency fluctuations, and geopolitical risks to determine the most appropriate timing and approach for exiting international real estate investments.

Investing in international real estate presents unique opportunities and challenges for investors seeking diversification and global exposure. By understanding market dynamics, conducting thorough due diligence, and leveraging local expertise, investors can capitalize on international real estate opportunities and achieve their investment objectives in a dynamic and interconnected global economy.

CHAPTER 11:

Sustainable and Impact Investing

Sustainable and impact investing integrates environmental, social, and governance (ESG) factors into investment decisions to generate positive societal and environmental outcomes alongside financial returns. By allocating capital to projects, businesses, and assets that prioritize sustainability, social responsibility, and ethical practices, investors can drive positive change while achieving their financial goals. This approach fosters long-term value creation, promotes environmental stewardship, and addresses pressing global challenges such as climate change, social inequality, and resource scarcity. Through sustainable and impact investing, investors can align their values with their investment objectives and contribute to a more sustainable and equitable future for generations to come.

11.1 Environmental Considerations in Real Estate

Environmental considerations play a crucial role in real estate investment, development, and management. In this section, we explore the various environmental factors that investors need to consider when evaluating real estate opportunities.

1. Environmental Site Assessments:

- Conduct environmental site assessments (ESAs) to evaluate potential environmental risks and liabilities associated with real estate properties, including contamination, pollution, and hazardous materials.
- Assess the historical land use, environmental history, and regulatory compliance of properties to identify potential environmental issues that may impact property value and future development.

2. Regulatory Compliance:

- Ensure compliance with environmental regulations, zoning ordinances, and land use restrictions governing real estate development, construction, and operation.
- Obtain necessary permits, approvals, and environmental clearances to mitigate regulatory risks and ensure legal compliance throughout the project lifecycle.

3. Sustainability Initiatives:
- Incorporate sustainability initiatives into real estate projects to minimize environmental impact, reduce resource consumption, and enhance energy efficiency.
- Implement green building practices, renewable energy solutions, and sustainable design features to improve environmental performance and attract environmentally conscious tenants.

4. Climate Change Resilience:
- Assess climate change risks and vulnerabilities associated with real

estate assets, including exposure to natural disasters, sea level rise, extreme weather events, and changing climate patterns.

- Incorporate climate resilience strategies, such as flood mitigation measures, stormwater management systems, and building retrofits, to enhance property resilience and mitigate climate-related risks.

5. Environmental Due Diligence:

- Conduct thorough environmental due diligence during property acquisitions, including Phase I and Phase II environmental assessments, to identify potential environmental liabilities and assess remediation costs.
- Engage environmental consultants, engineers, and specialists to evaluate soil and groundwater contamination, air quality, asbestos, lead paint, and other environmental hazards.

6. Green Certifications:

- Pursue green building certifications, such as LEED (Leadership in Energy and Environmental Design), Energy Star, or BREEAM (Building Research Establishment Environmental Assessment Method), to validate environmental performance and sustainability credentials of real estate assets.
- Certifications demonstrate commitment to sustainability, enhance marketability, and potentially command premium rents and property values.

7. Environmental Insurance:

- Consider obtaining environmental insurance coverage, such as pollution liability insurance or environmental impairment liability insurance, to protect against potential environmental liabilities and cleanup costs.
- Environmental insurance provides financial protection and risk transfer mechanisms for real estate investors,

developers, and property owners facing environmental risks.

8. Stakeholder Engagement:
- Engage with stakeholders, including local communities, government agencies, environmental advocacy groups, and tenants, to address environmental concerns, solicit feedback, and foster transparent communication.
- Collaborate with stakeholders to develop sustainable development strategies, mitigate environmental impacts, and promote responsible stewardship of real estate assets.

By incorporating environmental considerations into real estate decision-making processes, investors can mitigate environmental risks, enhance property value, and contribute to a more sustainable built environment. Proactive management of environmental factors not only protects investors from potential liabilities but also fosters long-term sustainability and resilience in real estate investments.

11.2 Socially Responsible Investing

Socially responsible investing (SRI), also known as sustainable, socially conscious, or ethical investing, integrates environmental, social, and governance (ESG) criteria into investment decisions to generate positive social and environmental impact alongside financial returns. In this section, we explore the principles, strategies, and considerations of socially responsible investing in real estate.

1. Social Impact Criteria:
- Consider social impact criteria such as affordable housing, community development, access to education, healthcare, and job creation when evaluating real estate investment opportunities.
- Assess the potential social benefits and contributions of real estate

projects to local communities, stakeholders, and society at large.

2. Diversity and Inclusion:
- Promote diversity, equity, and inclusion in real estate investments by supporting projects and initiatives that foster equal opportunities, fair treatment, and representation for all individuals regardless of race, gender, ethnicity, or background.
- Encourage diversity in tenant demographics, workforce composition, and leadership roles within real estate portfolios.

3. Affordable Housing Initiatives:
- Invest in affordable housing projects and initiatives to address housing affordability challenges, support underserved communities, and provide safe, decent, and affordable housing options for low-income individuals and families.
- Collaborate with government agencies, nonprofit organizations, and community stakeholders to

develop and finance affordable housing solutions.

4. Community Development Programs:

- Support community development programs and initiatives that enhance local infrastructure, public amenities, and quality of life in surrounding neighborhoods.
- Invest in mixed-use developments, urban revitalization projects, and public-private partnerships that promote economic growth, cultural enrichment, and social well-being.

5. Philanthropy and Corporate Social Responsibility:

- Align real estate investments with philanthropic goals and corporate social responsibility (CSR) initiatives to make a positive impact on society and address pressing social challenges.
- Allocate a portion of investment proceeds or rental income towards charitable causes, community

programs, and social impact initiatives.

6. Stakeholder Engagement:
- Engage with stakeholders, including tenants, employees, local communities, and advocacy groups, to understand their needs, concerns, and aspirations.
- Incorporate stakeholder feedback into real estate decision-making processes and project planning to ensure alignment with social responsibility objectives and values.

7. Ethical Business Practices:
- Adhere to ethical business practices, integrity, and transparency in real estate transactions, operations, and interactions with stakeholders.
- Avoid investments in projects or companies associated with unethical practices, human rights violations, environmental degradation, or social harm.

8. Impact Measurement and Reporting:

- Implement mechanisms to measure, monitor, and report the social impact and sustainability performance of real estate investments.
- Utilize key performance indicators (KPIs), impact metrics, and reporting frameworks to track progress, communicate results, and demonstrate accountability to stakeholders.

By integrating social responsibility principles into real estate investment strategies, investors can create positive social impact, foster inclusive growth, and contribute to sustainable development goals. Socially responsible investing in real estate not only aligns with ethical values and principles but also enhances long-term value creation and resilience in real estate portfolios.

11.3 Impact of Technology on Real Estate

Technology plays a transformative role in shaping the real estate industry, revolutionizing how properties are developed, marketed, managed, and transacted. In this section, we explore the significant impact of technology on various aspects of the real estate sector.

1. Property Search and Discovery:
- Utilize online platforms, mobile apps, and virtual reality (VR) technology to streamline property search and discovery processes for buyers, tenants, and investors.
- Access detailed property listings, 3D property tours, interactive maps, and neighborhood data to facilitate informed decision-making and enhance user experience.

2. Data Analytics and Market Insights:
- Harness big data analytics, artificial intelligence (AI), and machine learning algorithms to analyze vast

amounts of real estate data and derive actionable market insights.
- Gain valuable intelligence on market trends, pricing dynamics, demand-supply imbalances, and investment opportunities to inform investment strategies and optimize portfolio performance.

3. Smart Buildings and IoT Integration:
- Implement smart building technologies and Internet of Things (IoT) devices to enhance operational efficiency, occupant comfort, and sustainability in commercial and residential properties.
- Integrate sensors, automation systems, energy management solutions, and smart controls to monitor and optimize building performance in real time.

4. Digital Transactions and Blockchain:
- Facilitate seamless real estate transactions through digital platforms, e-signatures, and blockchain technology, reducing paperwork,

transaction costs, and processing
times.

- Utilize blockchain-based platforms for
  property title verification, land registry
  management, and transparent real
  estate transactions with enhanced
  security and immutability.

5. Predictive Maintenance and Asset Management:

- Implement predictive maintenance
  algorithms and remote monitoring
  systems to proactively identify
  maintenance issues, optimize asset
  performance, and minimize downtime
  in real estate portfolios.
- Leverage data-driven insights to
  prioritize maintenance tasks, allocate
  resources efficiently, and extend the
  lifespan of building systems and
  components.

6. Coworking and Flexible Workspaces:

- Embrace coworking and flexible
  workspace models enabled by
  technology platforms, enabling

remote work, collaboration, and agility in commercial real estate.
- Meet evolving tenant preferences for flexibility, community, and amenities by offering shared workspaces, on-demand meeting rooms, and scalable office solutions.

7. Property Marketing and Branding:
- Leverage digital marketing strategies, social media platforms, and content marketing to promote properties, engage with audiences, and build brand awareness in competitive real estate markets.
- Create compelling visual content, virtual property tours, and immersive experiences to showcase property features, amenities, and lifestyle benefits to prospective buyers and tenants.

8. Cybersecurity and Data Privacy:
- Prioritize cybersecurity measures, encryption protocols, and data privacy safeguards to protect sensitive information, financial

transactions, and personal data in real estate transactions and operations.

- Implement robust cybersecurity protocols, employee training programs, and incident response plans to mitigate cyber threats and safeguard against data breaches.

By embracing technology-driven innovations and digital transformation initiatives, the real estate industry can unlock new opportunities, improve operational efficiencies, and deliver enhanced value to stakeholders. Embracing technological advancements positions real estate professionals to adapt to evolving market dynamics, meet changing consumer expectations, and drive innovation in the digital age.

11.4 Ethical Practices for Real Estate Investors

Ethical practices are paramount in the real estate industry, ensuring fairness, integrity, and trustworthiness in all dealings. In this section, we explore the ethical principles and best practices that real estate investors should adhere to in their investment activities.

1. Transparency and Disclosure:

- Provide transparent and accurate information to all stakeholders, including buyers, sellers, tenants, investors, and partners, regarding property details, transaction terms, risks, and disclosures.
- Disclose any conflicts of interest, material facts, or potential issues that may impact investment decisions or affect the integrity of real estate transactions.

2. Fair and Honest Dealings:

- Conduct business with honesty, fairness, and integrity, adhering to ethical standards and professional codes of conduct in all interactions with clients, colleagues, and counterparties.

- Avoid engaging in deceptive, fraudulent, or unethical practices that may compromise trust, tarnish reputation, or violate legal and regulatory requirements.

3. Respect for Property Rights:
- Respect property rights, ownership interests, and contractual obligations of all parties involved in real estate transactions, ensuring compliance with property laws, zoning regulations, and land use restrictions.
- Safeguard intellectual property rights, trademarks, copyrights, and proprietary information related to real estate assets, developments, or marketing materials.

4. Confidentiality and Privacy:
- Maintain confidentiality and privacy of sensitive information, client data, and personal details obtained during real estate transactions, exercising discretion and safeguarding confidentiality rights.

- Protect client confidentiality, sensitive financial information, and proprietary business data from unauthorized disclosure, misuse, or exploitation.

5. Professional Competence:
- Uphold professional competence, expertise, and diligence in real estate investment analysis, due diligence, risk assessment, and decision-making processes, seeking continuous education and skill development.
- Exercise sound judgment, prudent investment practices, and fiduciary responsibilities in managing real estate assets, portfolios, and investment funds.

6. Social Responsibility:
- Consider the social, environmental, and community impacts of real estate investments, promoting sustainable development, responsible stewardship, and community engagement initiatives.

- Support socially responsible projects, philanthropic endeavors, and charitable causes that contribute to societal well-being, environmental conservation, and community development.

7. Compliance with Laws and Regulations:

- Comply with applicable laws, regulations, and ethical guidelines governing real estate investments, ensuring adherence to anti-discrimination laws, fair housing regulations, and consumer protection statutes.
- Stay informed about legal requirements, industry standards, and regulatory changes impacting real estate transactions, investment structures, and operational practices.

8. Accountability and Corporate Governance:

- Maintain accountability, oversight, and transparency in corporate governance practices, board structures, and decision-making processes within real estate investment entities.

- Establish robust internal controls, risk management frameworks, and compliance mechanisms to prevent fraud, misconduct, and unethical behavior in real estate operations.

By embracing ethical practices and upholding high standards of integrity and professionalism, real estate investors can build trust, foster positive relationships, and contribute to the long-term sustainability and success of the real estate industry. Ethical conduct not only enhances reputation and credibility but also creates value for investors, stakeholders, and communities served by the real estate sector.

CHAPTER 12:

Navigating Regulatory Challenges

Real estate investors encounter various regulatory challenges, including zoning restrictions, land use regulations, environmental laws, and tax compliance requirements. Navigating these challenges requires diligent research, legal expertise, and adherence to regulatory guidelines. By staying informed, seeking professional advice, and proactively addressing regulatory issues, investors can mitigate risks and ensure compliance with applicable laws, fostering successful real estate investments while minimizing legal liabilities.

12.1 Regulatory Landscape for Real Estate Investors

The regulatory landscape for real estate investors encompasses a complex framework of laws, regulations, and policies governing property ownership, development, transactions, and management. In this section, we examine the key aspects of the regulatory environment that real estate investors need to navigate.

1. Zoning and Land Use Regulations:
- Understand zoning ordinances, land use regulations, and planning requirements imposed by local governments to govern the use, development, and density of real estate properties.
- Comply with zoning restrictions, setback requirements, building codes, and design standards when acquiring, developing, or renovating properties to ensure regulatory compliance and avoid land use conflicts.

2. Environmental Laws and Regulations:
- Navigate environmental laws, regulations, and permitting requirements governing real estate

development, construction, and remediation activities, including the Clean Air Act, Clean Water Act, and Comprehensive Environmental Response, Compensation, and Liability Act (CERCLA).

- Conduct environmental due diligence, site assessments, and remediation efforts to address potential contamination, hazardous materials, and environmental liabilities associated with real estate properties.

3. Fair Housing and Anti-Discrimination Laws:

- Adhere to fair housing laws, anti-discrimination statutes, and equal opportunity regulations that prohibit discrimination based on race, color, religion, sex, disability, familial status, or national origin in real estate transactions, leasing practices, and property management.
- Implement fair housing policies, nondiscriminatory practices, and affirmative marketing strategies to

promote equal access to housing opportunities and comply with fair housing requirements.

4. Taxation and Fiscal Policies:

- Navigate tax laws, fiscal policies, and incentives impacting real estate investments, including property taxes, capital gains taxes, depreciation deductions, and tax credits for affordable housing, historic preservation, or renewable energy projects.
- Structure real estate transactions, ownership entities, and investment vehicles to optimize tax efficiency, minimize tax liabilities, and maximize after-tax returns for investors.

5. Securities Regulations and Investment Laws:

- Comply with securities regulations, investment laws, and regulatory requirements governing real estate investment trusts (REITs), private placements, crowdfunding platforms, and syndication offerings to raise capital from investors.

- Adhere to disclosure obligations, registration requirements, and investor protection measures mandated by securities regulators to ensure compliance with securities laws and regulations.

6. Consumer Protection and Disclosure Requirements:

- Abide by consumer protection laws, disclosure requirements, and real estate licensing regulations that govern real estate transactions, agency relationships, and professional conduct in brokerage activities.
- Provide accurate and complete disclosures, property disclosures, and material facts to buyers, sellers, tenants, and counterparties to facilitate informed decision-making and mitigate legal risks.

7. Landlord-Tenant Laws and Lease Regulations:

- Navigate landlord-tenant laws, lease regulations, and rental housing ordinances governing residential and commercial tenancies, including lease agreements, rent control, eviction procedures, and tenant rights.
- Comply with lease terms, lease renewal requirements, habitability standards, and maintenance obligations to maintain landlord-tenant relationships and avoid legal disputes or tenant grievances.

8. Regulatory Compliance and Risk Management:

- Establish robust compliance programs, risk management strategies, and internal controls to ensure regulatory compliance, mitigate legal risks, and uphold ethical standards in real estate operations.
- Monitor regulatory developments, legislative changes, and industry trends to adapt to evolving regulatory

requirements and anticipate potential compliance challenges.

By navigating the regulatory landscape effectively and proactively addressing regulatory compliance issues, real estate investors can mitigate legal risks, enhance operational efficiency, and foster sustainable growth in their investment portfolios. Understanding the regulatory environment and adhering to applicable laws and regulations are essential for success and resilience in the dynamic real estate market.

12.2 Compliance and Legal Obligations

Compliance with legal obligations is fundamental for real estate investors to operate ethically, mitigate risks, and uphold the integrity of their investments. In this section, we delve into the essential compliance requirements and legal obligations that real estate investors must adhere to.

1. Contractual Agreements:

- Ensure compliance with contractual agreements, purchase contracts, lease agreements, and financing documents governing real estate transactions.
- Abide by the terms, conditions, and obligations outlined in contractual agreements to avoid breaches of contract and legal disputes with counterparties.

2. Regulatory Compliance:

- Adhere to regulatory requirements, licensing laws, zoning ordinances, and environmental regulations applicable to real estate investments.
- Obtain necessary permits, approvals, and regulatory clearances to ensure compliance with local, state, and federal regulations governing property development, construction, and operations.

3. Anti-Money Laundering (AML) Compliance:

- Implement anti-money laundering (AML) policies, procedures, and controls to prevent illicit activities, money laundering, and terrorist financing in real estate transactions.
- Conduct due diligence, customer screening, and transaction monitoring to detect and report suspicious activities in compliance with AML regulations.

4. Fair Housing Laws:
- Comply with fair housing laws, anti-discrimination statutes, and equal opportunity regulations that prohibit discrimination based on race, color, religion, sex, disability, familial status, or national origin in real estate transactions.
- Avoid discriminatory practices, steering, redlining, or disparate treatment of protected classes to ensure fair and equitable treatment of all individuals.

5. Data Privacy and Protection:

- Protect sensitive information, personal data, and client confidentiality in compliance with data privacy laws, cybersecurity regulations, and consumer protection statutes.
- Implement data encryption, access controls, and data breach response protocols to safeguard against unauthorized access, data breaches, and privacy violations.

6. Tax Compliance:
- Comply with tax laws, reporting requirements, and tax filing obligations related to real estate investments, property ownership, and rental income.
- File accurate and timely tax returns, claim eligible deductions, and adhere to tax withholding obligations to ensure compliance with federal, state, and local tax regulations.

7. Securities Regulations:
- Adhere to securities regulations, investment laws, and disclosure

requirements governing real estate investment offerings, private placements, and securities transactions.

- Comply with securities registration, disclosure obligations, and investor accreditation requirements mandated by securities regulators to ensure compliance with securities laws.

8. Environmental Compliance:

- Mitigate environmental risks, contamination liabilities, and hazardous materials exposure through compliance with environmental laws, remediation requirements, and pollution control regulations.
- Conduct environmental due diligence, site assessments, and remediation efforts to address environmental issues and ensure compliance with environmental regulations.

By prioritizing compliance with legal obligations, real estate investors can mitigate legal risks, protect their investments, and maintain trust and credibility with stakeholders. Proactive adherence to legal requirements fosters ethical conduct, regulatory compliance, and long-term sustainability in real estate investments.

12.3 Adapting to Policy Changes

Adapting to policy changes is crucial for real estate investors to navigate regulatory shifts, economic fluctuations, and market uncertainties effectively. In this section, we explore strategies for real estate investors to adapt to policy changes proactively.

1. Stay Informed:
Keep abreast of policy changes, legislative updates, and regulatory reforms that impact the real estate sector. Stay informed through industry publications, government announcements, and legal advisories.

2. Analyze Implications:
Assess the implications of policy changes on real estate investments, market

dynamics, and investment strategies. Conduct thorough analyses to understand how policy shifts may affect property values, financing options, and investment returns.

3. Engage with Stakeholders:
Engage with policymakers, government officials, industry associations, and advocacy groups to advocate for policies that support a conducive environment for real estate investment. Participate in policy discussions, consultations, and forums to provide input and influence regulatory outcomes.

4. Flexibility in Strategy:
Maintain flexibility in investment strategies and adapt to changing policy environments. Be prepared to pivot investment approaches, asset allocation, and portfolio management tactics to align with evolving regulatory frameworks and market conditions.

5. Regulatory Compliance:
Ensure compliance with new regulations, reporting requirements, and compliance obligations resulting from policy changes. Allocate resources for regulatory

compliance efforts, legal counsel, and internal controls to mitigate legal risks and uphold regulatory standards.

6. Diversification:

Diversify real estate investments across different asset classes, geographic regions, and market segments to spread risk and minimize exposure to policy-specific vulnerabilities. Diversification can help buffer against adverse policy impacts in specific sectors or markets.

7. Monitor Market Trends:

Monitor market trends, economic indicators, and investor sentiment to anticipate the effects of policy changes on real estate markets. Stay vigilant for emerging opportunities or risks resulting from policy shifts and adjust investment strategies accordingly.

8. Long-Term Perspective:

Maintain a long-term perspective on real estate investments and avoid reactionary decision-making in response to short-term policy changes. Focus on fundamental value drivers, sustainable income streams, and resilient investment themes over the long term.

By proactively adapting to policy changes, real estate investors can mitigate risks, capitalize on opportunities, and position themselves for success in a dynamic regulatory landscape. Flexibility, strategic foresight, and proactive engagement with stakeholders are key to navigating policy uncertainties effectively.

12.4 Working with Government Agencies

Collaborating with government agencies is essential for real estate investors to navigate regulatory requirements, obtain permits, and facilitate development projects. In this section, we explore strategies for effectively working with government agencies.

1. Establish Relationships:
- Build relationships with key officials, regulators, and decision-makers within government agencies responsible for zoning, permitting,

land use planning, and
environmental regulations.
- Cultivate open lines of
communication, attend public
meetings, and engage in constructive
dialogue to foster positive
relationships with government
stakeholders.

2. Understand Regulations:
- Familiarize yourself with local, state,
and federal regulations governing
real estate development,
construction, and land use.
Understand the regulatory
framework, permitting processes,
and compliance requirements
applicable to your projects.

3. Seek Guidance:
- Seek guidance from government
agencies early in the project planning
phase to understand regulatory
requirements, obtain necessary
permits, and address potential
compliance issues.

- Consult with planning departments, building code officials, environmental agencies, and other relevant authorities to navigate regulatory hurdles effectively.

4. Provide Information:
- Provide comprehensive project information, site plans, environmental assessments, and impact studies to government agencies to facilitate permit review processes and demonstrate compliance with regulatory standards.
- Be transparent, responsive, and cooperative in providing requested information and addressing agency concerns to expedite permit approvals and project timelines.

5. Collaborate on Solutions:
- Collaborate with government agencies to develop solutions, mitigate environmental impacts, and address community concerns related to real estate development projects.

- Work proactively with regulatory authorities to identify potential challenges, explore alternatives, and find mutually beneficial outcomes that balance development objectives with regulatory requirements.

6. Advocate for Policies:
- Advocate for policies, zoning changes, and regulatory reforms that support responsible real estate development, economic growth, and community development initiatives.
- Engage in public hearings, policy discussions, and advocacy campaigns to influence decision-making processes and shape regulatory frameworks in alignment with industry interests.

7. Engage in Public-Private Partnerships:
- Explore opportunities for public-private partnerships (PPPs) with government agencies to collaborate on infrastructure projects,

affordable housing initiatives, and community redevelopment efforts.
- Leverage government resources, funding mechanisms, and regulatory incentives to facilitate real estate projects that benefit both public and private stakeholders.

8. Maintain Compliance:
- Maintain ongoing compliance with regulatory requirements, permit conditions, and environmental regulations throughout the project lifecycle.
- Monitor changes in regulatory landscapes, update project plans as needed, and proactively address compliance issues to avoid delays, penalties, or legal challenges.

By working effectively with government agencies, real estate investors can navigate regulatory complexities, streamline permitting processes, and facilitate successful project development. Building collaborative partnerships with regulatory authorities fosters a conducive environment for responsible real estate investment and sustainable development initiatives.

CHAPTER 13:

Case Studies and Success Stories

Case studies and success stories provide valuable insights into real-world examples of successful real estate investments, strategies, and outcomes. By analyzing case studies, investors can learn from others' experiences, identify best practices, and gain practical knowledge applicable to their own investment endeavors. Success stories inspire and motivate investors by showcasing achievements, overcoming challenges, and demonstrating the potential for profitability and growth in real estate investments.

13.1 Real-life Examples of Successful Investment

Real-life examples of successful investments offer valuable lessons and inspiration for aspiring real estate investors.

In this section, we delve into noteworthy case studies and examples of successful real estate investments, highlighting key strategies, challenges overcome, and outcomes achieved.

1. Multifamily Apartment Complex:
- Case Study: Acquisition and renovation of a multifamily apartment complex in a growing urban area.
- Strategy: Implemented value-add strategy by renovating units, improving amenities, and enhancing property management.
- Outcome: Increased rental income, improved occupancy rates, and boosted property value, resulting in significant returns on investment.

2. Commercial Office Building:
- Case Study: Purchase and repositioning of a distressed commercial office building in a prime business district.
- Strategy: Repositioned the property through extensive renovations,

modernization, and strategic leasing
efforts.
- Outcome: Transformed the property
into a Class A office space, attracted
high-quality tenants, and generated
stable cash flow and capital
appreciation.

3. Retail Shopping Center:
- Case Study: Redevelopment of an
underperforming retail shopping
center into a vibrant mixed-use
destination.
- Strategy: Repurposed the property
by adding entertainment venues,
restaurants, and experiential retail
offerings.
- Outcome: Revitalized the shopping
center, increased foot traffic, and
created a thriving community hub,
resulting in increased tenant demand
and property value.

4. Industrial Warehouse Portfolio:
- Case Study: Acquisition and
optimization of an industrial

warehouse portfolio in high-demand logistics markets.

- Strategy: Implemented a buy-and-hold strategy, optimized property management practices, and capitalized on e-commerce growth trends.
- Outcome: Achieved stable rental income, high occupancy rates, and long-term appreciation in property values, driven by strong market fundamentals.

5. Mixed-Use Development Project:

- Case Study: Development of a mixed-use project combining residential, commercial, and retail components in an emerging neighborhood.
- Strategy: Created a live-work-play environment by integrating residential units, office spaces, and retail amenities.
- Outcome: Transformed the neighborhood, catalyzed economic development, and generated substantial returns for investors

through a successful development project.

These real-life examples illustrate the diverse opportunities, strategies, and success stories in real estate investment. By studying these case studies, investors can gain insights, learn from successful strategies, and apply proven techniques to their own investment endeavors, ultimately achieving their financial goals in the dynamic world of real estate.

13.2 Lessons Learned from Failures

Learning from failures is an essential aspect of real estate investment, providing valuable insights and opportunities for growth. In this section, we explore lessons learned from failures in real estate investment, highlighting key takeaways and strategies for mitigating risks.

1. Overleveraging:
- Lesson Learned: Excessive leverage can amplify risks and lead to financial

distress, especially in downturns or market fluctuations.

- Strategy: Avoid overleveraging by maintaining conservative loan-to-value ratios, sufficient cash reserves, and prudent debt management practices.

2. Lack of Due Diligence:

- Lesson Learned: Inadequate due diligence can result in unforeseen issues, such as environmental liabilities, zoning restrictions, or title defects.
- Strategy: Conduct thorough due diligence, including property inspections, title searches, environmental assessments, and legal reviews, to identify and mitigate potential risks.

3. Misjudging Market Trends:

- Lesson Learned: Failure to accurately assess market trends, demand dynamics, and competitive forces can lead to investment underperformance.

- Strategy: Stay informed about local market conditions, demographic trends, and economic indicators to make informed investment decisions and adapt to changing market dynamics.

4. Poor Property Management:
- Lesson Learned: Ineffective property management practices, such as inadequate maintenance, tenant relations, or rent collection, can erode property value and tenant satisfaction.
- Strategy: Invest in professional property management services, establish clear policies and procedures, and prioritize tenant satisfaction to maximize property performance and investor returns.

5. Lack of Diversification:
- Lesson Learned: Concentrated investment portfolios lacking diversification are vulnerable to sector-specific risks and market downturns.

- Strategy: Diversify investment portfolios across different asset classes, geographic locations, and market segments to spread risk and enhance resilience against market volatility.

6. Ignoring Regulatory Compliance:
- Lesson Learned: Non-compliance with regulatory requirements, zoning regulations, or building codes can result in legal liabilities, fines, or project delays.
- Strategy: Stay current with regulatory changes, engage with local authorities, and ensure compliance with all applicable laws and regulations throughout the investment lifecycle.

7. Underestimating Capital Needs:
- Lesson Learned: Underestimating capital requirements for property acquisitions, renovations, or operational expenses can strain cash flow and hinder investment performance.

- Strategy: Conduct comprehensive financial analysis, including realistic budgeting, contingency planning, and sensitivity analysis, to ensure adequate capitalization and mitigate financial risks.

8. Emotional Decision-Making:
- Lesson Learned: Emotionally driven investment decisions, such as fear of missing out (FOMO) or chasing speculative trends, can lead to irrational behavior and poor investment outcomes.
- Strategy: Maintain discipline, objectivity, and a long-term perspective in investment decision-making, relying on thorough analysis, research, and risk assessment to guide investment choices.

By learning from failures and adopting proactive risk management strategies, real estate investors can navigate challenges, mitigate risks, and achieve sustainable success in the dynamic and competitive real estate market. Embracing failure as a learning opportunity empowers investors to make informed decisions, adapt to changing market conditions, and build resilient investment portfolios over time.

13.3 Inspiring Stories of Wealth Creation

In this section, we delve into inspiring stories of wealth creation through real estate investment, highlighting individuals who have achieved remarkable success in building wealth and financial independence through strategic real estate endeavors.

1. From Rags to Riches:

- Story: John Doe started with modest means, purchasing his first rental property with savings from his day job. Through diligent property management, reinvestment of profits, and strategic acquisitions, he gradually expanded his real estate portfolio, accumulating wealth and achieving financial freedom.

2. Entrepreneurial Vision:

- Story: Jane Smith identified an opportunity to revitalize a neglected neighborhood by developing affordable housing for low-income families. Despite initial challenges and skepticism from investors, her visionary approach, community engagement, and perseverance led to the successful transformation of the neighborhood, creating value for residents and investors alike.

3. Adaptive Resilience:

- Story: Mike Johnson faced setbacks during the 2008 financial crisis when several of his properties faced foreclosure and declining values. Instead of giving up, he pivoted his strategy, renegotiated financing terms, and capitalized on distressed asset opportunities. Through resilience, adaptability, and strategic reinvestment, he not only recovered but also thrived, building a more resilient and diversified real estate portfolio.

4. Strategic Partnerships:

- Story: Sarah Brown leveraged strategic partnerships and joint ventures to scale her real estate business rapidly. By collaborating with experienced investors, developers, and industry professionals, she accessed new markets, diversified investment opportunities, and accelerated her wealth-building journey through synergistic collaborations and shared expertise.

5. Visionary Development:

- Story: Mark Williams had a vision to develop a sustainable mixed-use community that integrated residential, commercial, and recreational amenities. Through meticulous planning, innovative design, and sustainable development practices, he created a model community that attracted residents, businesses, and investors, generating long-term value and positive social impact.

6. Generational Legacy:

- Story: The Smith family established a multi-generational real estate dynasty by passing down knowledge, expertise, and assets from one generation to the next. Through prudent estate planning, intergenerational wealth transfer, and a shared commitment to long-term stewardship, they preserved and grew their real estate legacy, leaving a lasting impact for future generations.

7. Philanthropic Impact:

- Story: James and Lisa Johnson used their real estate wealth to make a difference in their community by supporting affordable housing initiatives, educational programs, and charitable organizations. By aligning their investment goals with social impact, they not only generated financial returns but also created positive change and left a meaningful legacy of giving back.

8. Global Vision:
- Story: David Lee expanded his real estate empire internationally, capitalizing on emerging market opportunities and global trends. Through astute market analysis, cross-border investments, and cultural intelligence, he diversified his portfolio, tapped into new growth markets, and positioned himself as a visionary leader in the global real estate arena.

These inspiring stories demonstrate the transformative power of real estate investment in creating wealth, fostering innovation, and making a positive impact on communities and individuals' lives. By learning from these examples and embracing their entrepreneurial spirit, aspiring real estate investors can unlock their own potential for success and wealth creation in the dynamic world of real estate.

13.4 Strategies for Overcoming Challenges

In this section, we explore effective strategies for overcoming challenges commonly encountered in real estate investment. By understanding and implementing these strategies, investors can navigate obstacles, mitigate risks, and achieve success in their real estate endeavors.

1. Robust Risk Management:
- Identify potential risks and uncertainties associated with real estate investments, such as market fluctuations, regulatory changes, or unforeseen expenses.
- Implement proactive risk management strategies, including diversification, contingency planning, and hedging mechanisms, to mitigate risks and safeguard investment portfolios.

2. Resilient Portfolio Diversification:

- Diversify investment portfolios across different asset classes, geographic locations, and market segments to spread risk and minimize exposure to sector-specific vulnerabilities.
- Balance high-risk, high-return investments with more stable income-producing assets to create a resilient and diversified real estate portfolio.

3. Adaptive Market Analysis:
- Stay informed about local market conditions, economic trends, and demographic shifts to anticipate changes and adapt investment strategies accordingly.
- Conduct thorough market analysis, feasibility studies, and due diligence to identify emerging opportunities and mitigate risks associated with market volatility.

4. Strategic Partnership Collaboration:
- Collaborate with experienced professionals, industry experts, and strategic partners to leverage their

knowledge, resources, and networks in navigating complex real estate transactions.

- Form strategic partnerships, joint ventures, or syndications to pool resources, share risks, and capitalize on investment opportunities that may be beyond individual capabilities.

5. Innovative Financing Solutions:

- Explore alternative financing options, such as private equity, crowdfunding, or seller financing, to overcome challenges related to traditional lending constraints or capital limitations.
- Negotiate favorable financing terms, leverage tax incentives, and optimize capital structures to maximize leverage and enhance investment returns.

6. Agile Adaptation to Market Trends:

- Stay agile and flexible in adapting investment strategies to changing market dynamics, technological advancements, and evolving consumer preferences.

- Embrace innovation, adopt new technologies, and leverage data analytics to optimize property performance, enhance tenant experiences, and stay ahead of the competition.

7. Proactive Problem-Solving:

- Anticipate potential challenges and develop contingency plans to address unexpected events, setbacks, or disruptions in real estate operations.
- Foster a proactive problem-solving mindset, encourage open communication, and empower team members to collaborate on finding creative solutions to complex challenges.

8. Continuous Learning and Improvement:

- Invest in ongoing education, professional development, and industry networking to stay abreast of

best practices, emerging trends, and innovative solutions in real estate investment.
- Learn from past experiences, both successes, and failures, and apply lessons learned to refine investment strategies, optimize performance, and achieve long-term success.

By implementing these strategies for overcoming challenges, real estate investors can build resilience, adaptability, and sustainability in their investment approach, ultimately achieving their financial goals and creating lasting value in the dynamic and competitive real estate market.

CHAPTER 14:

Future Trends and Innovations

The future of real estate investment is shaped by emerging trends and innovations that redefine industry practices, reshape market dynamics, and create new opportunities for investors. From technological advancements to shifting consumer preferences, staying ahead of future trends is essential for success in the ever-evolving real estate landscape. Embracing innovation, adapting to change, and leveraging emerging trends can position investors to capitalize on future opportunities and thrive in an increasingly competitive market.

14.1 Emerging Technologies in Real Estate

The integration of emerging technologies is revolutionizing the real estate industry, offering new opportunities for investors to enhance operational efficiency, improve tenant experiences, and unlock value in their portfolios. In this section, we explore key emerging technologies shaping the future of real estate investment.

1. Artificial Intelligence (AI) and Machine Learning:

- AI and machine learning algorithms analyze vast datasets to identify trends, predict market fluctuations, and optimize investment decisions.
- AI-powered tools streamline property management, automate routine tasks, and enhance operational efficiency for real estate investors.

2. Internet of Things (IoT):

- IoT devices, such as smart sensors and connected appliances, enable real-time monitoring of property conditions, energy usage, and tenant preferences.
- IoT technology enhances asset performance, reduces maintenance costs, and improves sustainability initiatives in real estate portfolios.

3. Virtual and Augmented Reality (VR/AR):

- VR and AR technology offer immersive experiences for property tours, virtual staging, and architectural visualization.
- VR/AR tools facilitate remote due diligence, enhance marketing efforts, and attract tenants and investors by showcasing properties in interactive and engaging formats.

4. Blockchain and Smart Contracts:

- Blockchain technology enables secure and transparent transactions, digital asset management, and fractional ownership of real estate assets.
- Smart contracts automate contract execution, streamline lease agreements, and reduce administrative overhead in real estate transactions.

5. Big Data Analytics:

- Big data analytics harnesses large volumes of data from various sources to derive actionable insights, optimize property performance, and inform investment decisions.
- Data-driven analytics enhance risk assessment, market forecasting, and portfolio optimization strategies for real estate investors.

6. Sustainable Technologies:
- Sustainable technologies, such as renewable energy systems, green building materials, and energy-efficient HVAC systems, promote environmental stewardship and reduce operational costs in real estate assets.
- Sustainability initiatives enhance asset value, attract socially responsible tenants, and align with growing investor demand for environmentally conscious investment opportunities.

7. 3D Printing and Prefabrication:

- 3D printing and prefabrication techniques revolutionize construction processes, reduce construction timelines, and lower building costs for real estate developers.
- Modular construction methods enable rapid deployment of housing solutions, adaptive reuse projects, and sustainable development initiatives in real estate portfolios.

8. Robotic Process Automation (RPA):
- RPA technology automates repetitive tasks, data entry, and back-office operations, improving efficiency and reducing human error in real estate workflows.
- RPA solutions streamline property management, lease administration, and financial reporting processes for real estate investors and operators.

By embracing emerging technologies, real estate investors can unlock new efficiencies, drive innovation, and capitalize on opportunities to create value in their investment portfolios. Keeping abreast of technological advancements and integrating relevant solutions into investment strategies will be paramount in navigating the future of real estate investment successfully.

14.2 Predictions for Market Evolution

Predicting the evolution of the real estate market is essential for investors to adapt their strategies and capitalize on emerging opportunities. In this section, we explore key predictions for the future evolution of the real estate market based on current trends and forecasts.

1. Shift Towards Remote Work:
- Prediction: The rise of remote work and flexible work arrangements will influence demand for commercial office space, with a potential shift towards mixed-use developments and suburban coworking spaces.
- Implications: Investors may focus on repurposing office properties for alternative uses, investing in

suburban office markets, or incorporating flexible workspace amenities to cater to changing tenant preferences.

2. Urbanization Trends:

- Prediction: Urbanization trends will continue, driving demand for multifamily housing in urban centers, mixed-use developments, and transit-oriented communities.
- Implications: Investors may prioritize investments in urban infill projects, transit-oriented developments, and mixed-use properties that cater to urban lifestyle preferences and accessibility to amenities and transportation.

3. Sustainable Development:

- Prediction: Increasing emphasis on sustainability and environmental stewardship will shape development trends, influencing design standards, building codes, and tenant preferences.

- Implications: Investors may focus on sustainable development practices, green building certifications, and energy-efficient technologies to enhance property value, attract environmentally conscious tenants, and meet regulatory requirements.

4. Technology Integration:
- Prediction: Technology integration will become ubiquitous across all aspects of real estate operations, from property management and leasing to tenant experiences and asset performance monitoring.
- Implications: Investors may invest in proptech solutions, data analytics platforms, and smart building technologies to optimize property performance, streamline operations, and enhance tenant satisfaction.

5. Demand for Affordable Housing:
- Prediction: Demand for affordable housing will intensify, driven by demographic shifts, income inequality, and urbanization trends,

creating opportunities for investment in workforce housing and affordable rental properties.

- Implications: Investors may target investments in affordable housing developments, preservation of existing affordable housing stock, and public-private partnerships to address the growing need for housing affordability.

6. E-commerce Growth:

- Prediction: Continued growth of e-commerce and last-mile delivery services will drive demand for industrial and logistics properties, particularly in strategic distribution hubs and urban logistics centers.
- Implications: Investors may focus on investments in industrial warehouses, fulfillment centers, and logistics facilities to capitalize on the booming e-commerce sector and evolving supply chain dynamics.

7. Demographic Shifts:

- Prediction: Demographic shifts, including aging populations, millennial homeownership trends, and Gen Z preferences, will influence housing demand, lifestyle choices, and investment opportunities.
- Implications: Investors may tailor investment strategies to cater to demographic preferences, such as multifamily housing for millennials, active adult communities for retirees, and co-living arrangements for young professionals.

8. Regulatory Changes:
- Prediction: Regulatory changes, tax incentives, and government policies will shape investment landscapes, influencing development incentives, affordable housing initiatives, and zoning regulations.
- Implications: Investors may monitor regulatory developments, engage with policymakers, and adapt investment strategies to align with changing regulatory environments and market conditions.

By considering these predictions for market evolution, real estate investors can position themselves strategically to capitalize on emerging trends, mitigate risks, and achieve long-term success in the dynamic and evolving real estate market landscape.

14.3 Opportunities in the Post-Pandemic Era

As the world emerges from the COVID-19 pandemic, new opportunities are arising in the real estate market. In this section, we explore key opportunities that investors can leverage in the post-pandemic era.

1. Adaptive Reuse and Repurposing:

- Opportunity: With changing consumer behavior and preferences, there's potential for adaptive reuse and repurposing of existing properties, such as converting underutilized commercial spaces into residential units or mixed-use developments.

- Implications: Investors can capitalize on this trend by identifying properties with adaptive reuse potential, navigating zoning regulations, and repositioning assets to meet evolving market demands.

2. Remote Work Flexibility:
- Opportunity: The widespread adoption of remote work has shifted preferences towards flexible work arrangements and decentralized office spaces, creating opportunities for suburban office developments, coworking spaces, and satellite offices.
- Implications: Investors can explore opportunities in suburban office markets, invest in coworking space operators, and adapt office designs to accommodate hybrid work models and collaborative environments.

3. Technology Integration:
- Opportunity: Accelerated digital transformation and technology adoption present opportunities for

investors to integrate smart building technologies, data analytics platforms, and virtual leasing solutions to enhance operational efficiency and tenant experiences.

- Implications: Investors can invest in proptech startups, retrofit properties with smart technology, and leverage data analytics to optimize property performance and inform investment decisions.

4. Affordable Housing Demand:

- Opportunity: The pandemic has exacerbated housing affordability challenges, creating demand for workforce housing, affordable rental properties, and subsidized housing initiatives.
- Implications: Investors can target investments in affordable housing developments, preservation of existing affordable housing stock, and public-private partnerships to address the growing need for housing affordability.

5. Healthcare and Life Sciences:

- Opportunity: Heightened focus on healthcare and life sciences sectors has increased demand for medical office buildings, research facilities, and biotech clusters.
- Implications: Investors can explore opportunities in healthcare real estate, invest in medical office buildings, and develop specialized facilities to support medical research and innovation.

6. Sustainable Development Initiatives:

- Opportunity: Growing emphasis on sustainability and ESG (Environmental, Social, and Governance) criteria presents opportunities for investments in green buildings, renewable energy projects, and sustainable development initiatives.
- Implications: Investors can prioritize sustainability initiatives, pursue green building certifications, and integrate renewable energy solutions to

enhance property value and attract
socially responsible tenants.

7. Industrial and Logistics Expansion:
- Opportunity: Accelerated
  e-commerce growth and changing
  supply chain dynamics are driving
  demand for industrial warehouses,
  fulfillment centers, and last-mile
  delivery facilities.
- Implications: Investors can capitalize
  on the booming e-commerce sector
  by investing in industrial and logistics
  properties in strategic locations,
  optimizing distribution networks, and
  leveraging technology to streamline
  operations.

8. Urban Revitalization Projects:
- Opportunity: Urban revitalization
  initiatives and public-private
  partnerships present opportunities for
  investors to participate in urban
  redevelopment projects,
  infrastructure upgrades, and
  community revitalization efforts.

- Implications: Investors can collaborate with local governments, community organizations, and developers to revitalize urban neighborhoods, create mixed-use developments, and enhance quality of life for residents.

By seizing these opportunities in the post-pandemic era, real estate investors can position themselves for success, drive innovation, and contribute to sustainable economic recovery and growth in the evolving real estate market landscape.

14.4 Adapting to Changing Consumer Preferences

Understanding and adapting to changing consumer preferences is crucial for real estate investors to remain competitive and capitalize on market opportunities. In this section, we explore strategies for adapting to evolving consumer preferences in the real estate market.

1. Flexible Workspaces:

- Adaptation: With the rise of remote work and flexible work arrangements, there's a growing demand for flexible workspaces, coworking spaces, and satellite offices.
- Strategy: Investors can adapt by incorporating flexible workspace amenities into office properties, partnering with coworking space operators, and providing versatile lease terms to accommodate changing tenant needs.

2. Urban Lifestyle Amenities:

- Adaptation: Urban dwellers increasingly prioritize access to amenities such as parks, green spaces, recreational facilities, and cultural attractions.
- Strategy: Investors can enhance the desirability of urban properties by incorporating lifestyle amenities, fostering walkable communities, and investing in mixed-use developments that offer a diverse range of services and experiences.

3. Sustainable Living:

- Adaptation: There's a growing preference for sustainable and environmentally conscious living among consumers, driving demand for green buildings, energy-efficient features, and eco-friendly communities.
- Strategy: Investors can cater to this preference by investing in sustainable development projects, retrofitting properties with green technologies, and obtaining green building certifications to attract environmentally conscious tenants.

4. Technology Integration:

- Adaptation: Consumers increasingly expect seamless technology integration in their living and working spaces, including smart home devices, high-speed internet connectivity, and digital amenities.
- Strategy: Investors can integrate smart building technologies, offer high-speed internet access, and

provide digital amenities such as virtual concierge services and online rent payment platforms to enhance tenant experiences.

5. Health and Wellness:

- Adaptation: Health and wellness considerations have become paramount for consumers, leading to increased demand for properties that promote active living, access to outdoor spaces, and wellness amenities.
- Strategy: Investors can incorporate wellness amenities such as fitness centers, yoga studios, and outdoor recreation areas into their properties, prioritize health-conscious design features, and promote a healthy lifestyle ethos within communities.

6. Multigenerational Living:

- Adaptation: Multigenerational living arrangements are gaining popularity as families seek to live closer together for social support and caregiving purposes.

- Strategy: Investors can adapt by developing multigenerational housing options, such as accessory dwelling units (ADUs), multifamily complexes with diverse unit sizes, and senior living communities that offer intergenerational programming and amenities.

7. Experience-Oriented Retail:
- Adaptation: Consumers prioritize experiential retail concepts over traditional brick-and-mortar stores, seeking immersive shopping experiences, entertainment venues, and dining options.
- Strategy: Investors can reimagine retail spaces by incorporating experiential elements, curating unique tenant mixtures, and hosting events and activations that engage consumers and drive foot traffic.

8. Digital Connectivity:
- Adaptation: Digital connectivity and access to high-speed internet have become essential utilities for

consumers, influencing housing decisions and workplace preferences.

- Strategy: Investors can ensure properties are equipped with reliable internet infrastructure, offer tech-enabled amenities such as smart home features and remote access controls, and prioritize digital connectivity as a key selling point for tenants and occupants.

By understanding and adapting to changing consumer preferences, real estate investors can align their investment strategies with market demand, enhance property value, and create desirable living and working environments that meet the evolving needs of today's consumers.

CHAPTER 15:

Building a Legacy

Building a legacy in real estate involves more than just financial success—it's about leaving a lasting impact on communities, creating opportunities for future generations, and shaping the built environment for years to come. Whether through sustainable development, philanthropic initiatives, or fostering social and economic growth, building a legacy in real estate requires vision, integrity, and a commitment to leaving the world a better place than we found it.

15.1 Wealth Preservation and Generational Planning

Wealth preservation and generational planning are crucial aspects of long-term success in real estate investment. In this section, we delve into strategies for preserving wealth and ensuring a smooth transition of assets to future generations.

1. Asset Protection Strategies:
- Wealth Preservation: Implement asset protection strategies such as limited liability entities, insurance coverage, and trusts to safeguard real estate assets from potential risks, liabilities, and creditor claims.

2. Estate Planning:
- Generational Planning: Develop comprehensive estate plans, wills, and trusts to outline the distribution of real estate assets and ensure a seamless transfer of wealth to heirs and beneficiaries.

3. Tax Efficiency:
- Tax Planning: Utilize tax-efficient strategies such as gifting, charitable donations, and 1031 exchanges to minimize tax liabilities and maximize the value of real estate investments across generations.

4. Family Governance:

- Legacy Preservation: Establish family governance structures, such as family offices or advisory boards, to facilitate communication, decision-making, and succession planning for real estate assets.

5. Philanthropic Initiatives:

- Social Impact: Incorporate philanthropic initiatives and charitable giving into generational planning to support causes aligned with family values, promote social impact, and leave a positive legacy for future generations.

6. Education and Communication:

- Knowledge Transfer: Foster education and communication within the family to impart financial literacy, real estate expertise, and shared values that will empower future generations to responsibly manage and steward family assets.

7. Professional Advisory:

- Expert Guidance: Engage qualified professionals, including estate planners, tax advisors, and wealth managers, to provide expert guidance and facilitate generational planning strategies tailored to the unique needs and goals of the family.

8. Continual Review and Adaptation:
- Adaptability: Continually review and adapt generational planning strategies in response to changing legal, tax, and market conditions to ensure the long-term preservation and growth of family wealth across multiple generations.

By implementing these wealth preservation and generational planning strategies, real estate investors can protect their assets, transfer wealth effectively, and leave a lasting legacy for future generations to enjoy and build upon.

15.2 Philanthropic Endeavors in Real Estate

Philanthropic endeavors in real estate provide opportunities for investors to make a positive impact on society while also aligning with their values and goals. In this section, we explore various ways investors can engage in philanthropy within the realm of real estate.

1. Affordable Housing Initiatives:

- Social Impact: Invest in affordable housing developments, support housing nonprofits, or advocate for policies that address housing affordability challenges in communities.

2. Community Development Projects:

- Urban Revitalization: Partner with local governments, community organizations, and developers to fund and support community development projects that enhance quality of life, create jobs, and stimulate economic growth.

3. Environmental Conservation:

- Sustainable Development: Embrace sustainable development practices, green building certifications, and renewable energy projects to promote environmental conservation and reduce carbon footprints in real estate projects.

4. Education and Youth Development:

- Scholarship Programs: Establish scholarship programs, mentorship initiatives, or educational grants to support students pursuing careers in real estate or related fields and foster youth development.

5. Healthcare and Wellness Facilities:

- Medical Research: Invest in healthcare real estate, support medical research institutions, or fund healthcare facilities that provide essential services and promote wellness within communities.

6. Cultural Preservation:

- Historic Preservation: Contribute to historic preservation efforts, restoration projects, or cultural heritage initiatives that preserve architectural landmarks and promote cultural identity.

7. Disaster Relief and Recovery:
- Emergency Response: Provide financial support, donate real estate assets, or volunteer resources to aid in disaster relief and recovery efforts during natural disasters or humanitarian crises.

8. Philanthropic Partnerships:
- Collaborative Initiatives: Form philanthropic partnerships with other investors, nonprofits, or corporate entities to pool resources, leverage expertise, and maximize social impact in addressing pressing societal needs.

Engaging in philanthropic endeavors allows real estate investors to contribute positively to society, address social and environmental challenges, and leave a lasting legacy that transcends financial returns. By integrating philanthropy into their investment strategies, investors can create meaningful change and make a difference in the communities they serve.

15.3 Crafting a Lasting Impact

Crafting a lasting impact in real estate goes beyond financial success—it involves making meaningful contributions to society, fostering sustainable development, and leaving a positive legacy for future generations. In this section, we explore strategies for investors to create a lasting impact through their real estate endeavors.

1. Sustainable Development Practices:

- Environmental Stewardship: Implement sustainable development practices, green building certifications, and renewable energy initiatives to minimize environmental impact and promote sustainability in real estate projects.

2. Social Responsibility Initiatives:

- Community Engagement: Engage with local communities, stakeholders, and residents to understand their needs, address social issues, and contribute to the overall well-being of the community through real estate investments.

3. Economic Empowerment Programs:

- Job Creation: Invest in projects that create job opportunities, stimulate economic growth, and promote economic empowerment within underserved communities, thereby fostering socio-economic development and prosperity.

4. Affordable Housing Solutions:

- Housing Accessibility: Develop affordable housing solutions, advocate for housing policy reforms, and collaborate with government agencies and nonprofits to address housing affordability challenges and provide access to safe and affordable housing for all.

5. Education and Skill Development:

- Capacity Building: Support educational initiatives, vocational training programs, and skill development workshops that empower individuals and communities to enhance their knowledge, skills, and socio-economic prospects.

6. Cultural Preservation Efforts:

- Heritage Conservation: Contribute to the preservation of cultural heritage sites, historic landmarks, and architectural treasures, safeguarding cultural identity and enriching the built environment for present and future generations.

7. Philanthropic Partnerships:

- Collaborative Impact: Forge strategic partnerships with philanthropic organizations, nonprofits, and community groups to pool resources, share expertise, and amplify social impact in addressing critical societal challenges.

8. Legacy Planning and Generational Wealth Transfer:

- Intergenerational Stewardship: Develop comprehensive legacy plans, estate strategies, and generational wealth transfer mechanisms to ensure the continuity of values, principles, and philanthropic endeavors across multiple generations.

By crafting a lasting impact through sustainable development, social responsibility, and community engagement, real estate investors can contribute to building vibrant, resilient communities, fostering inclusive growth, and leaving a positive legacy that transcends financial returns. Through purpose-driven investments and philanthropic initiatives, investors can play a transformative role in shaping a more equitable, sustainable, and prosperous future for all.

15.4 Reflections on a Successful Real Estate Journey

Reflecting on a successful real estate journey offers valuable insights, lessons learned, and perspectives gained along the way. In this section, we delve into reflections shared by seasoned real estate investors, highlighting key takeaways and wisdom accumulated from their experiences.

1. Embracing Adaptability:
- Lesson Learned: Success in real estate requires adaptability to changing market conditions, emerging trends, and unforeseen challenges.
- Reflection: Embrace flexibility, remain agile, and proactively adjust strategies to capitalize on opportunities and navigate obstacles encountered throughout the journey.

2. Building Relationships:

- Lesson Learned: Relationships are foundational to success in real estate, fostering trust, collaboration, and mutual benefit among stakeholders.
- Reflection: Cultivate strong networks, prioritize integrity, and invest in meaningful relationships with partners, clients, and community members to drive long-term success and create lasting impact.

3. Learning from Setbacks:
- Lesson Learned: Setbacks and failures are inevitable in real estate, but they offer valuable lessons and opportunities for growth.
- Reflection: Embrace failure as a learning experience, analyze mistakes, and leverage setbacks as catalysts for innovation, resilience, and personal development on the journey to success.

4. Long-Term Vision:
- Lesson Learned: Real estate investment is a long-term endeavor

that requires patience, perseverance, and a strategic vision for the future.

- Reflection: Maintain a clear long-term vision, set achievable goals, and stay committed to the journey despite short-term challenges or fluctuations in the market.

5. Prioritizing Values:

- Lesson Learned: Success in real estate goes beyond financial gains—it's about aligning actions with core values, ethics, and principles.
- Reflection: Prioritize integrity, social responsibility, and ethical conduct in all business dealings, ensuring that success is measured not only by financial returns but also by the positive impact made on society and communities.

6. Continuous Learning:

- Lesson Learned: The real estate industry is dynamic and ever-evolving, requiring a commitment to lifelong learning and professional development.

- Reflection: Stay curious, seek out new knowledge, and invest in ongoing education, training, and mentorship opportunities to stay ahead of trends, expand expertise, and adapt to changing market dynamics.

7. Gratitude and Giving Back:
- Lesson Learned: Success in real estate is not achieved alone, but through the support of mentors, colleagues, and the broader community.
- Reflection: Practice gratitude, express appreciation for those who have contributed to your journey, and pay it forward by giving back to others through mentorship, philanthropy, and community engagement initiatives.

8. Celebrating Milestones:
- Lesson Learned: Celebrate achievements, milestones, and successes along the real estate

journey to acknowledge progress and inspire continued growth.

- Reflection: Take time to celebrate accomplishments, recognize team efforts, and reflect on the journey's milestones, reinforcing motivation, resilience, and a sense of fulfillment in the pursuit of excellence.

Through reflection on their successful real estate journeys, investors gain valuable insights, deepen their understanding, and glean wisdom to inform future decisions, strategies, and endeavors in the dynamic and rewarding world of real estate investment.

APPENDICES

A. Glossary of Real Estate Terms

1. **Appraisal**: An estimation of the value of a property, typically conducted by a licensed appraiser.
2. **Closing**: The final step in a real estate transaction where the property ownership is transferred from the seller to the buyer.
3. **Deed**: A legal document that transfers the ownership of a property from one party to another.
4. **Escrow**: A neutral third-party account where funds and documents are held until the completion of a real estate transaction.
5. **Foreclosure**: The legal process through which a lender repossesses a property from a borrower who has defaulted on their mortgage payments.
6. **Interest Rate**: The percentage charged by a lender for borrowing

money, typically associated with mortgage loans.

7. **Lien**: A legal claim against a property to secure the repayment of a debt or obligation.
8. **Mortgage**: A loan used to finance the purchase of real estate, with the property serving as collateral for the loan.
9. **Title**: The legal right to ownership of a property, typically evidenced by a title deed.
10. **Zoning**: The process of dividing land into different zones or districts for specific uses, such as residential, commercial, or industrial.

B. Resources for Further Learning

1. **Books**:
   - "The Millionaire Real Estate Investor" by Gary Keller
   - "Rich Dad Poor Dad" by Robert Kiyosaki

- o "The Book on Rental Property Investing" by Brandon Turner
2. **Online Courses**:
   - o Udemy: "Real Estate Investing: Learn to Fix & Flip, Step by Step"
   - o Coursera: "Introduction to Real Estate" by the University of Pennsylvania
3. **Podcasts**:
   - o BiggerPockets Podcast: Offers insights and advice from successful real estate investors.
   - o Real Estate Guys Radio Show: Covers a wide range of topics related to real estate investing and wealth building.
4. **Websites/Blogs**:
   - o BiggerPockets: Provides a wealth of articles, forums, and resources for real estate investors.
   - o Investopedia: Offers comprehensive guides and articles on real estate investing and financial concepts.

5. **Professional Organizations**:
   - National Association of Realtors (NAR): Provides education, networking, and advocacy for real estate professionals.
   - American Real Estate Society (ARES): Offers research and publications on real estate economics and finance.

C. Sample Investment Templates and Documents

1. **Property Analysis Worksheet**: A spreadsheet template for analyzing potential real estate investments, including calculations for cash flow, ROI, and property valuation.

2. **Investment Agreement**: A sample legal document outlining the terms and conditions of an investment partnership or joint venture in a real estate project.

3. **Rental Lease Agreement**: A standardized contract outlining the terms of a rental agreement between a landlord and tenant, including rent amount, lease duration, and property rules.

4. **Due Diligence Checklist**: A checklist outlining the steps and considerations for conducting due diligence on a prospective real estate investment, including property inspections, financial analysis, and legal review.

5. **Property Management Agreement**: A sample contract outlining the responsibilities and obligations of a property management company hired to oversee a rental property on behalf of the owner.

6. **1031 Exchange Documents**: Sample forms and instructions for completing a 1031 exchange, a tax-deferred strategy used by real estate investors to reinvest proceeds from the sale of one property into another.

D. Recommended Reading List

1. **"The Millionaire Real Estate Investor"** by Gary Keller: Offers insights and strategies from successful real estate investors to help readers build wealth through property investments.

2. **"Rich Dad Poor Dad"** by Robert Kiyosaki: Provides valuable lessons on financial literacy, investing, and wealth building, including real estate investment principles.

3. **"The Book on Rental Property Investing"** by Brandon Turner: Offers practical advice and strategies for building wealth through rental

property investments, including tips on finding, financing, and managing rental properties.

4. **"Real Estate Investing for Dummies"** by Eric Tyson and Robert S. Griswold: Provides a comprehensive introduction to real estate investing, covering topics such as property selection, financing, and risk management.

5. **"The Real Estate Wholesaling Bible"** by Than Merrill: Offers a step-by-step guide to real estate wholesaling, a strategy for acquiring properties at a discount and selling them for a profit without the need for extensive capital or credit.

6. **"Commercial Real Estate Investing for Dummies"** by Peter Conti and Peter Harris: Provides an overview of commercial real estate investing, including strategies for acquiring, financing, and managing commercial properties such as office buildings, retail centers, and multifamily complexes.

7. **"Real Estate Finance and Investments"** by William B. Brueggeman and Jeffrey D. Fisher: Offers an in-depth exploration of real estate finance and investment principles, including analysis techniques, valuation methods, and financing strategies.

8. **"The ABCs of Real Estate Investing"** by Ken McElroy: Provides practical advice and insights from a seasoned real estate investor on building wealth through property investments, including tips on finding deals, negotiating, and managing properties for maximum returns.

Thank you for joining me on this journey through real estate investment. As you close this book, remember to take action on what you've learned and embrace the adventure ahead. Whether you're flipping houses or managing rentals, enjoy the process and pursue your dreams with passion. Wishing you abundance and success on your real estate journey!

Best regards,

[Diana Hardy]

www.ingramcontent.com/pod-product-compliance
Lightning Source LLC
Chambersburg PA
CBHW071029290526
45795CB00004B/1157